PEOPLE SKILLS FOR ENGINEERS

Tony Munson

Copyright © 2018 by Tony Munson

All rights reserved. Written permission must be secured from the author to use or reproduce any part of this book, except for brief quotations in critical reviews or articles.

The author may be contacted through his website at www.peopleskillsforengineers.com.

ISBN: 9781723996788

To all the engineers who want to be more skillful with people, but don't know where to start, this book is for you.

Contents

Preface ix

Acknowledgments xv

Introduction xvii

Chapter 1: Why People Skills Are So Important to Engineers 1

    Team Effectiveness 2

    Money and Promotions 3

    Future Opportunities 6

    Technical Ability Is Only Part of Your Success 10

    Better Health 12

Chapter 2: Landing the Job 17

    Surviving the Phone Screen 19

    Preparing for the On-Site Interview 21

    Tips for the Day of the On-Site Interview 24

Chapter 3: Joining an Existing Team 29

Chapter 4: Dealing with Management 37

    Getting Along with Your Manager 38

    If You Want to Impress Your Manager, Do These Things 42

Chapter 5: Dealing with Difficult Engineers 49

    Are You a Difficult Engineer? 50

    Establish a Rapport 54

    Learn Their Communication Style 55

    Sometimes You Have to Give In 56

    Keep Difficult People Out of Your Organization in the First Place ... 57

Chapter 6: Leading Technical Teams 61

    Why Should People Want to Follow You? 63

    Connect with People First 64

    Listen First, Then Decide 68

    "I'm Not Tony Stark" 70

Chapter 7: How to Avoid and Resolve Conflict 73

    We Have a "Bank Account" with Other People 75

    You Reap What You Sow 77

    Think about What You Say Before You Say It 79

    Don't Criticize or Complain 80

    Forgive People When They Do Stupid Things 84

    Admit Your Mistakes and Apologize, If Necessary 86

    Ask Questions to Avoid Unnecessary Conflict 88

    Refuse to Be Offended 90

    Don't Argue 91

Chapter 8: Appreciate People and Make Them Feel Important 97

    Appreciation Motivates People 98

    Appreciation Should Be a Lifestyle 100

    Tangible Gifts 101

Initiate Interactions with People 103
Chapter 9: Get to Know Others 107
    What's Important to Them? 108
    Make Yourself Available 109
    If You Want to Be Liked, Be Likeable 110
    The Power of Lunch 112
Chapter 10: Names. Yup, They're That Important 115
    Just Ask 116
    Demonstrate People Are Important to You 117
    Names Personalize Interactions 118
    The Million-Dollar Test 119
    Tips for Remembering More Names 120
Chapter 11: How to Correct People 125
    Does It Matter If They Are Wrong? 126
    Correct People in Private, If Possible 128
    Focus on the Behavior, Not the Person 130
    Cushion the Blow 131
Chapter 12: How to Be a Better Listener 135
    Are You Really Listening? 136
    Listen with Your Body 137
    Don't Interrupt 140
    Demonstrate You Understand 141
    Don't Hijack the Conversation 142
Chapter 13: Design and Code Reviews 145
    Face-to-Face Reviews Are Best 146
    Code: It Is Personal 147
    Don't Be Overly Critical 148

Ways to Approach Correction 150
Chapter 14: Running a Productive Meeting 155
Do You Really Need a Meeting? 156
Before the Meeting 157
During the Meeting 159
After the Meeting 161
Chapter 15: Talking to Non-Technical People 163
Chapter 16: Mentorship 169
Why Mentoring Is Good for Your Company 170
If You Don't Have a Mentor, Get One 171
If You've Ever Considered Being a Mentor, Do It 173
Tips for Being a Great Mentor 175
Conclusion 179
Afterword 183
Bibliography 185

Preface

Have you ever had the feeling that you were doing something wrong, but couldn't quite put your finger on what? This is exactly how I used to feel as I tried to figure out why some personal interactions didn't turn out like I thought they should or why there seemed to be bad blood between myself and certain individuals for no obvious reason. To make matters worse, I had no idea how to go about fixing these problems once I thought I understood where I went wrong. In short, things seemed too dang hard, and I wanted to know why this was the case.

As I began to investigate the topic of people skills, it quickly became apparent to me that I had stumbled upon one of the foundational skill sets to living a happier, healthier, and more successful life. And this is coming from a technical guy. Initially, I was a little angry. I wondered: Where had this information been all my life? Why was this the first time I was seeing it? Turns out, I wasn't the only one who missed the memo on people skills.

As I began to grow, I immediately noticed that my fellow engineers could be better positioned for success if they learned the same thing

I was learning: how to *properly* interact with others. More specifically, how they could avoid and resolve conflicts, deal with offensive individuals, build stronger relationships to increase opportunities, and have a healthier influence over others, just to name a few.

Most high schools and colleges don't teach engineers what they need to know in this area, consequently, many of us are *grossly* unprepared to deal with the people problems we inevitably have to face not only on the job, but after we clock out for the day and go home. Because we aren't being taught these skills as part of our core engineering curriculum, some may assume they will come naturally. People skills are not typically innate in many engineers, so we are forced to take personal responsibility for our own development by proactively seeking out the training we need. This is where I come in.

"That's great, but who the @#$% are you?" you ask. I'm one of you—a software engineer. I hold a bachelor of science in computer science and have more than sixteen years of software engineering experience under my belt. I've worked in large and small research and development (R&D) groups. I write design documentation, submit code for review, and work on features, defects, and customer escalations. I attend daily stand-ups, weekly staff meetings, and have one-on-ones with my manager. During my career, I have helped develop custom Application-Specific Integrated Circuits (ASICs) with computer engineers and developed Linux drivers in C. I have developed infrastructure in .NET, designed mobile applications in Java and Objective-C, and implemented back-end server logic in Python. I've spent my entire career working with electrical engineers, computer engineers, mechanical engineers, and computer scientists, so I know *exactly* what it's like to grind it out year after year in a cube, working with difficult people.

Many engineers believe that the only thing that really matters is their ability to solve technical problems. Because of this, engineers can be socially lazy and may fail to understand how much their underdeveloped people skills costs them in lost opportunities (i.e., promotions, jobs, and work assignments), reduced efficiency, increased stress, and ultimately, their happiness. This ignorance keeps them blind to pursuing growth in this area. Additionally, many engineers have no idea what being good with people looks like in practice. With so few role models, it's the proverbial blind leading the blind in many work environments.

Successfully dealing with people is a skill set that engineers can develop over time and with use, but it can be tempting to give up when things get challenging. It's not uncommon for engineers to stop trying to improve in this area and withdraw into themselves, relying on hope and luck when it comes to interpersonal interactions. This is not a formula for success any more than relying on hope and luck when implementing your next technical deliverable.

Learning the correct way to do things can save a ton of frustration and anguish. As an engineer, you are a person first and an engineer second. Focusing on being a strong engineer before focusing on being a mature person is akin to putting the cart before the horse—you're getting things out of order. Your people skills, or lack thereof, bleed into every relationship and every interaction you have. If you have gaps in your core set of skills, you could potentially have *serious* problems. If you build your career on a strong foundation, many problems will never materialize. You will have avoided them completely.

People are very predictable. When we do things that are known to cause problems, there should be no surprise whatsoever when that's exactly what we get in return—more problems. We can learn where the land mines are and avoid them.

Engineers need help. With my background, I realized I could be the one to step in and fill the gap in this often neglected but critically important space. I want to give my fellow engineers more tools to use, so they can stop struggling with the same frustrating problems year after year. These problems include but are not limited to:

- Feeling isolated and disconnected from others.
- Problems with management or co-workers.
- Poor performance at interviews or meetings.

- Interaction regret or wishing they would have behaved differently in personal interactions.
- Inability to properly lead and motivate others.

What you are holding in your hands is the result of literally hundreds of hours of reading, teaching, mentoring, studying, and hands-on application. I spent years doing a deep dive into this type of material, so you don't have to. I distilled a lot of information down to pill-size form, keeping only what I considered the best parts. Each chapter and section was specifically selected because of the usefulness of the principles it contains. Every attempt was made to remove filler.

I'm a results kind of guy. If something isn't helping me, at best it's doing nothing for me, which means it needs to be evaluated. At worst, it's hurting me, and in that case, it needs to go. I not only found all the concepts in this book to be helpful from a personal standpoint, but also from a teaching perspective—they are changing people's lives. There is no theory here. Everything I'm going to tell you, I do myself. To the best of my ability, I tried to keep the material actionable and to the point.

There are reoccurring themes and scenarios that we all must deal with while working alongside other engineers and engineering managers. What I've put together is a resource that outlines the minimum core set of people skills every engineer needs to know to survive and thrive in the workplace. Why make people learn the hard way, through repeated failures, when their careers are on the line? If you're anything like me, you'd rather learn from someone else's mistakes rather than make the same mistakes yourself and potentially sabotage important opportunities along the way. My intent is that an engineer accepting a position at a company would be given this book and told: "Read this. It will save you a lot of personal agony and grief."

I tried to make the information accessible and relevant to every technical worker. Most of the information in this book transcends a specific engineering field, and the concepts can easily be applied to the situations you face in your specific discipline. Since I'm a software engineer, the material in this book naturally has a slant toward that discipline, and my years developing software have no doubt influenced my examples and experiences. Look for the similarities and then tweak the material as necessary.

Acknowledgments

I would like to thank the following individuals for their help and guidance in making this book. Without them, the material wouldn't be as complete as it is, and it would probably read like a fourth-grader wrote it.

> *Stephanie, my wife*—Writing a book takes a lot of time and energy. Stephanie is supportive of my desire to help others and has, on more than one occasion, talked me off the proverbial ledge when things got overwhelming. She has strengths that complement me perfectly.
>
> *Matt Messinger*—Matt is an architect where I work who has been very supportive of my activities since I first ran the idea past him years ago. His constructive feedback and encouragement along the way kept me believing that I was on to something big that could significantly help others in our fields. Matt is proof that words of encouragement really can have a dramatic impact on others.

James Penick—*James is a friend and co-worker who has helped me since the very beginning. Any time I ran material past him, he'd always have insightful feedback on how to make it better. James (and Matt) kept me from going off into the weeds and helped me keep the material focused and useful.*

Introduction

Be honest with yourself. When you hear the phrase "people skills," your first reaction (after rolling your eyes and sighing), may be similar to one of the following:

a. I'm *already* good with people. I don't need any more training.
b. I'm an engineer. I don't need people skills.
c. I'm not good with people, so I try to avoid them.

If you most closely identified with (a) above, you may be like I used to be: confused about what it means to be truly good with people. Looking back, I'm embarrassed at how little I actually knew when I started out. I had no idea how large the topic was, or how important people skills were to my career and my life. Because of my ignorance, I thought I'd already arrived and didn't need any additional help. I couldn't have been more wrong.

The phrase "people skills" leaves a lot of room for interpretation. If you think having strong people skills simply means you're an extrovert with a bubbly personality, you'll want to keep reading, because it's a much bigger and more important topic than that.

Businessdictionary.com defines people skills as "a set of skills enabling a person to get along with others, to communicate ideas effectively, to resolve conflicts, and to achieve personal or business goals. People skills are essential for business functions such as sales, marketing, and customer service, but are also important for all employees to ensure the smooth functioning of an organization."

People skills are a universally applicable, *learned* set of skills related to successfully managing your interactions and relationships with others. They are about understanding core human nature and using that knowledge to be happier, more productive, and more helpful to those around you. Any area of your life that involves interacting with another human being can benefit from having better people skills. Since your life is inextricably tied to others, *everyone* is in the people business, whether you choose to accept it or not. No one operates on an island completely disconnected from others. What you do affects other people for better or for worse. Why not get better at the game you already have to play?

People skills are one of the foundational skill sets that everyone needs to possess. They underpin all of your personal and professional endeavors. There is not a single area of your life that cannot be improved by being more skillful with people. Les Giblin, author of *Skill with People*, wrote, "Your skill with people determines the quality of your business life, your family life, and your social life." If you haven't intentionally grown your skills in this area or applied the skills you *have* learned, you're leaving a large percentage of your happiness, fulfillment, and financial success on the table.

Can you experience some success in life by being a completely self-centered egomaniac? Yes, you can, but you will also create significant collateral damage along the way, which will prevent you from experiencing the very best life has to offer. Success should be measured by how close we come to our potential, not where we stand relative to others.

Many engineers identify with (b) because they like to think their jobs are somehow different than other job functions like sales, marketing, and advertising. In reality, they are not. At the core of every job, teams of *people* push toward a goal *together*. As a team member, you either live or die as a unit. *People* schedule the work, implement the work, sell the work, and support the work, among many other activities. Since people are the primary vehicle for getting work done, it stands to reason that the healthier people and teams are physically and emotionally, the better their output will be. Individuals with poor people skills create barriers in organizations and have a negative impact on a team's overall effectiveness. Who hasn't purposefully avoided working with someone because they didn't want to deal with their abrasive personality? Those types of things nickel-and-dime your organization to death from a productivity standpoint.

Let there be no mistake about it: Company culture starts with *you*. It's not management's responsibility to make your company the best place to work, it's yours. If you want a fun, encouraging, and respectful work environment, be that way in all your small daily interactions. You have a very real and tangible impact on your company's culture. You make other people's time at your company better or worse. Do you really want an adversarial work environment where everyone is looking out for their own best interests and trying to one-up each other? All that produces is avoidance, isolation, fear, reduced productivity, disconnected team members, self-centered decision making, and increased turnover. Talk is cheap. Show that your work culture is important to you by taking personal ownership of your interactions. This isn't an either-or proposition. You can be an effective engineer *and* be skillful with people.

When mentoring software engineers, I tell them that people have an Application Programming Interface (API). In the software world, an API specifies how software components should interact with each other. People are similar to software. If you use their API incorrectly, you won't get the desired results. It's not their fault—you're the one using them incorrectly. Sadly, many of us violate people's APIs daily, and then wonder why things aren't running as smoothly as they should. You may work with imperfect people who can be stubborn and opinionated, especially engineers. How you engage them makes *all* the difference. Do it incorrectly, you get bad results. Do it correctly, you get better results.

If (c) resonated with you the most, don't fret. There's hope! A lot of people are not born with great people skills. The good news is that most people skills can be learned and have *nothing* to do with your ability to look or act comfortably in social settings. Those are small bonuses compared to some of the core skills we'll cover. One thing is for sure, you do have far more potential locked inside you than you think. With a little training, it will come out. Will you completely change overnight? No, but if you make it a habit of applying the principles in this book, your interactions with people will improve, and any movement in the right direction is a good thing.

Like anything else in life, the results you get will be proportionate to the amount of effort you put in. If you read this book, pat yourself on the back and say, "Wow, that sure was a nice read," then go right back to the way you've currently been interacting with people, you will see very little benefit. If you decide to change, and I'll do my best to convince you that you should, you *will* see a tangible improvement in your daily interactions at work and at home. Things will just start to work better because you'll be removing behaviors that are *known* to cause relational friction.

What do you want your *real* legacy to be? With few exceptions, regardless of how technically gifted you are, you *are* replaceable. Your influence on others is the only thing that outlives you. When you leave your company, what do you want people to say about you? What are you leaving behind? I'm going to challenge you to think bigger.

This book has rubber-meets-the-road practical advice for becoming better with people, and as a result, you will become a more effective engineer and create fewer problems for yourself and others. The following chapters contain tools and a concrete plan of action you can start using today. You may already be experiencing problems with your team members or your manager. After reading this book, you'll have some proven options to improve those situations.

Knowing is not the same as *doing.* Napoleon Hill, author of *Think and Grow Rich,* said: "Knowledge is only potential power. It becomes power only when, and if, it is organized into definite plans of action, and directed to a definite end." That's a powerful statement. Many people seem to believe knowledge is power, but that isn't entirely true. It's only power *if* it's used.

What does that mean for you? It means doing nothing with what you know is equivalent to not knowing it. The tips and tools in this book aren't going to do you any good until you decide to do something with them. Don't stop at knowing. Follow through with action.

As you go through this book, I'd like to encourage you to adopt an "eat the meat and spit out the bones" attitude. "Eat the meat" means to put into practice the principles that make sense to you, and "spit out the bones" means to disregard the things you disagree with. If you wholeheartedly disagree with something I've written after legitimately considering it, that's fine. Move on. Don't miss out on concepts that have the potential to positively impact some of the difficult relationships in your life simply because you disagreed with an issue earlier in the book.

Personally, I like to put the phrase "I may be wrong" high up on my list of responses when I'm encountering new information, especially material that's trying to stretch and grow me. Correction can sting a little at first, and this is normal. No one likes reading about how their behavior may have been adversely affecting their interactions with others, possibly for decades. I encourage you to fight through this initial sting and thoughtfully consider the information I'm presenting. Look for ways to apply it to your interactions with others.

Lastly, I've really tried my best to include helpful information with regards to the most common situations all engineers deal with. Not only have I included many chapters on fundamental people skills, but I also included a considerable amount of information on some of the very practical aspects of engineering, such as interviewing for a job, design and code reviews, conducting meetings, and getting along with your manager, just to name a few. I've done my best to give you something you can use this very day to make your career more productive and enjoyable. If you find the material in this book half as rewarding as I have, I will consider it a success. Enjoy!

CHAPTER 1
Why People Skills Are So Important to Engineers

Your success as an engineer is a combination of your "hard" (technical) and "soft" (people, leadership ability, etc.) skills. Engineers are not one-dimensional beings who are somehow exempt from the consequences of making poor decisions in areas not directly related to technical subjects. It is entirely possible to be a competent, effective engineer and end up having a lackluster career because you've habitually mismanaged other areas of your profession that depend on the successful application of a different kind of (non-technical) skill set.

To reach the highest levels of success in your career, you'll also need to be adept at dealing with people. This concept may be challenging for some of you because you think your technical skills are far and away the most important thing, and nothing is even a close second. This mindset can be difficult to overcome because many engineers have been incorrectly conditioned to focus almost exclusively on technical subject matter their entire adult life—they are out of balance.

In order to improve, every engineer should be willing to admit that they might be able to increase their effectiveness by focusing on developing other areas within themselves. If you think you're already doing everything right, you won't even consider trying something differently.

TEAM EFFECTIVENESS

In 2012, Google started an investigation into building the perfect team called Project Aristotle. After years of research, data analysis, and millions of dollars, they released the results of their investigation. The summary of their findings stated that "Of the five key dynamics of effective teams that the researchers identified, psychological safety was by far the most important. The Google researchers found that individuals on teams with higher psychological safety are less likely to leave Google, they're more likely to harness the power of diverse ideas from their teammates, they bring in more revenue, and they're rated as effective twice as often by executives."

Psychological safety is defined as "a shared belief that the team is safe for interpersonal risk taking. It can be defined as 'being able to show and employ one's self without fear of negative consequences of self-image, status or career.' In psychologically safe teams, team members feel accepted and respected." To gauge the psychological safety of a team, Google asked team members how strongly they agreed or disagreed with the following statements:

- If you make a mistake on this team, it is often held against you.
- Members of this team can bring up problems and tough issues.
- People on this team sometimes reject others for being different.
- It is safe to take a risk on this team.
- It is difficult to ask other members of this team for help.
- No one on this team would deliberately act in a way that

undermines my efforts.
- Working with members of this team, my unique skills and talents are valued and utilized.

Based on the nature of the statements, the effectiveness of a team is *not* based solely on the application of technical knowledge. Other factors appear to have a significant impact on team effectiveness as well. If we want our teams to be more successful, it's important that we do our part to ensure they are psychologically safe for its members, too.

Many of the traits of an effective and psychologically safe team are tied directly to the ability of its members to communicate effectively, encourage other team members, and value people. Since Google already did the research, we may as well take advantage of the findings. If we're trying to increase our team's effectiveness, and thus our company's effectiveness, without putting any emphasis on psychological safety, we might be passing up some easy productivity gains. To ignore the results of the research would be folly.

Later chapters are full of *specific* ways you can contribute to your team's safety and help harness more of your team's untapped effectiveness. Obviously, there is no substitute for raw talent. Anyone trying to convince you otherwise is peddling snake oil. The skills covered in this book are meant to complement the existing technical foundation most engineers already possess. I'm *not* suggesting they are a replacement—you can't hug your way out of a hard technical problem.

MONEY AND PROMOTIONS

Do you want to make more money and get promoted more quickly? If so, get better with people. On multiple occasions in my career, my people and leadership skills put me in the next higher performance bracket, which gave me an increased pay raise and performance bonus. That's money in my pocket, and it came by simply setting aside time to develop myself in other areas I was *already using,* albeit poorly.

Spending time developing your people skills will result not only in increased happiness, which can be difficult to prove to others since they aren't inside your head, but can result in additional income, which is not tough to prove at all. Strong people skills can set you apart from others in your peer group, which gives you an advantage during performance reviews. As Senior Software Engineer David Hitchcock put it, "You could be the most brilliant engineer and have a lackluster career if you cannot intelligently promote your product and skills via effective communication."

Your formal performance review may contain sections used to rate your communication and leadership skills. If you *are* being rated on leadership and communication skills, that says at least two things about where you work:

1. They are important to your company.
2. They factor in to your overall evaluation and have a direct impact on the rewards and recognition you'll receive.

Those two reasons alone should be enough incentive to pursue growth in these areas. Ignoring them is equivalent to saying, "I'm fine with getting 80 percent on any exam I ever take. I'm not even going to pursue the other 20 percent." But then, of course, you'd be the first to complain that you never seem to get anything above an 80 percent. Sounds ridiculous, right? Instead, shoot for the full 100 percent and get all the promotions, pay raises, and bonuses you're qualified to receive. You can't always control how much money is available for pay raises and bonuses, but don't give management reasons *not* to give them to you. When there are rewards available, you want your name in the discussion.

Exciting career opportunities, pay raises, and promotions don't fall from the sky. They are controlled by people. These people have biases, motives, and sometimes difficult personalities. If you think that simply keeping your head down and working hard is going to bring you the best life has to offer, you are fooling yourself.

Since *people* control many of the resources we are after, ignoring the criteria they are using to make decisions about who to give the resources to would be foolish. These people are the gatekeepers, and the better we are with the gatekeepers, the closer we are to whatever resources they control. This doesn't mean using any sort of manipulation or mind games, but that you recognize the traits (character, communication, work ethic, etc.) these people are looking for and then make sure you're meeting the mark in these areas. If your company is looking to promote someone into a position that requires excellent communication skills and you don't have them, you're not going to get the job because you don't possess the required skills.

If you're from the Nintendo Generation like me, you probably grew up playing a lot of video games. The early Nintendo games always seemed to have some sort of boss monster at the end of each level that you'd have to defeat to go on to the next level of the game. Life is sort of this way. There is typically a "boss" (gatekeeper) that must be figuratively defeated to unlock that next great opportunity in your life. This doesn't happen by force; instead, you must become more skilled technically and socially, so the gatekeeper of that opportunity will say, "Yes, you can have my business," or "Yes, let's give them a promotion."

It's also worth noting that the higher you go in an organization, more is expected from you with regards to your people skills. If you aspire to move up the corporate ladder, growing yourself in leadership and people skills will pay you back in increased opportunities and dollars. People who have the ability to promote you are actively looking for these traits.

There are some engineers reading this book who are frustrated because they are repeatedly passed up for promotions and feel like they are at their wits end on how to become more promotable. I recommend you take a closer look at your people skills. Have you put *any* effort into this area, or are you just hoping that one day you'll eventually make the cut? Take control of the situation. There are principles you can apply this very moment to start making yourself more appealing to the people who can give you the opportunities you're after.

FUTURE OPPORTUNITIES

The Opportunity Tree (fig. 1) is a powerful concept with the potential to significantly increase the number and quality of opportunities available to you throughout your career. In a nutshell, it's taking the concept of networking one step further to help you visualize the importance of relationships in your life. The Y circle at the bottom represents you, and all the P circles are the connections you have with other people. Although greatly oversimplified, the Opportunity Tree shows the people you have a direct connection to, and the people they have a connection to, and so on. The O stars are opportunities available to you through a specific relationship. These can be opportunities such as an interesting project, a new job, or investment capital for your new start-up, or anything. First-tier relationships are the people you personally know, and second-tier relationships are friends-of-a-friend connections. The process repeats far beyond the third tier but is capped there for practical reasons.

The little fire and the box around the branch on the right demonstrate what happens when you mismanage a relationship with a person at work or in your personal life. When you torch the relationship, you lose that entire branch of the tree. Not only do you miss any opportunities available through that person, but you also miss any opportunities available through the people that person knows. You shut down an entire network of people when you don't practice the skills necessary to cultivate, fix, or manage the relationship with the first-tier individual. And it doesn't stop there. Those people on the right branch also have connections to other people in your tree.

You've likely seen these connections play out in your life. Have you ever asked for a recommendation concerning someone who does a certain type of work and received the feedback, "I heard bad things about that person"? This is the Opportunity Tree in action. Somewhere

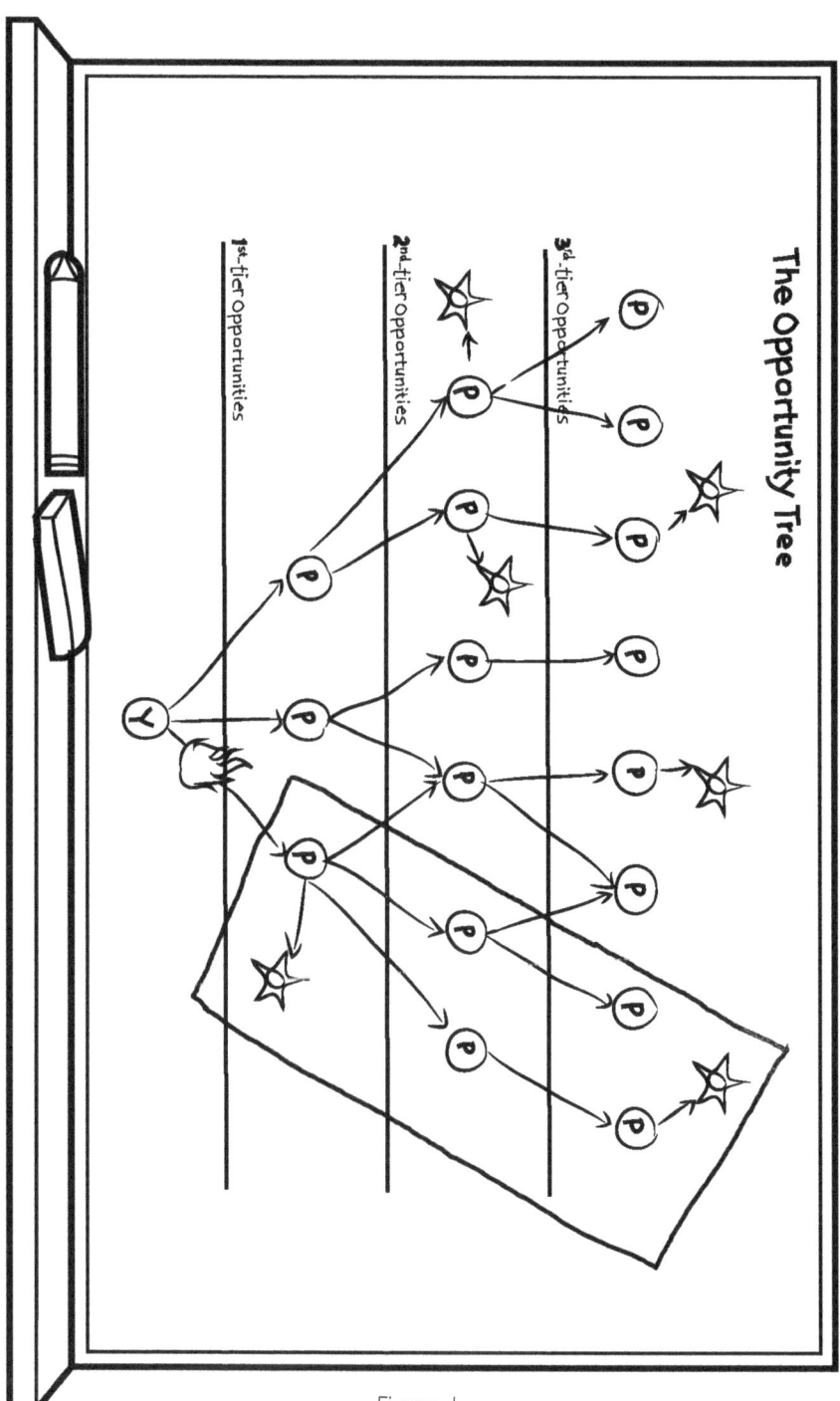

Why People Skills Are So Important to Engineers 7

Figure 1

along the line, that individual (the worker) had a negative interaction with someone else, and you're hearing about it. Negative interactions can kill opportunities in your life. What's worse, many times you don't even know it's happening. By mishandling personal interactions, you can burn off entire sections of your tree and greatly reduce future opportunities.

You may have been part of interview wrap-up meetings where you've discussed candidates for open positions and someone spoke up and said: "I'm not sure I'd hire him. I've worked with him before, and he can be really difficult." It's the Opportunity Tree again. Someone potentially missed an opportunity because they mismanaged a relationship somewhere along the line.

How did your current job opportunity become available to you? Were you blindly submitting resumes to companies on the Internet? Did a friend or acquaintance tell you about the specific position? When a company has positions to fill, typically its current employees start asking each other for referrals because it's one of the quickest ways to weed out unqualified candidates. If you were contacted because of one of these referrals, congratulations! Your relationship with another person opened up an opportunity for you. People typically will not recommend you if they don't like you, even if you have solid technical abilities. You'll miss out on the opportunity without ever knowing you were passed over.

This happens behind the scenes everywhere. Decisions are made about your future, and you don't even know they are happening. Developing your people skills will help with these types of situations because people won't be passing you up due to reservations about your ability to operate in a particular setting. Don't let your lack of skill with people disqualify you from opportunities.

Where do you want to be in ten years? Are you stacking the deck in your favor or putting the odds against you based on how you interact with other people? Those opportunities depend on the relationships you make *today*. As a personal testimony, a previous manager of mine contacted me about my current position after she moved on to another company. If I had mismanaged my relationship with her, I wouldn't be where I am today. I had also previously worked with some of the individuals on the interview team, which made it a much easier decision to hire me. They liked me as a person *and* liked the work I did. Had I been condescending, combative, and egotistical with these people in the past, I wouldn't be writing this book right now.

What else does the Opportunity Tree show? It shows that if you want more opportunities, you need to build out your tree by adding more branches to it. This is completely under your control. You can proactively build your tree as full as you want it, provided you possess the necessary skills to add healthy relationships as new limbs. If you don't feel like you have the opportunities that other people have, you might want to look at your tree. Do you have enough branches? Do you have any healthy branches at all? If not, this could be the source of your problems. You may not need more technical knowledge specific to your career; you may need more healthy relationships to unlock all those second- and third-tier connections and opportunities.

If you're like some people, you might get a little nervous hearing about the Opportunity Tree because you don't consider yourself to be a people person. The thought of having to build this big tree with lots of people in it might seem overwhelming to you. It's true that you will need to stretch yourself a little to grow your tree effectively, but throughout the rest of this book are tools to help you reach more people. If you're a bad conversationalist, there are tips for you. If you're not sure how to properly correct other people when they make mistakes, there are ideas for that too. Just decide that having a larger tree and all the opportunities that come with it is worth pursuing.

Don't just protect your current tree; proactively build out a bigger one. It's important to make sure your current connections with people are healthy, but focusing only on existing relationships will limit the overall size of your tree. Every chance you get, use your newfound abilities to proactively add entire new branches to your tree and watch the opportunities in your life begin to steadily increase over time.

TECHNICAL ABILITY IS ONLY PART OF YOUR SUCCESS

In Dale Carnegie's book *How to Win Friends and Influence People,* he stated that only 15 percent of a person's financial success is due to technical knowledge and about 85 percent is due to "human engineering" (interpersonal and leadership skills). These statistics were based on *A Study of Engineering Education* by Charles Riborg Mann, which was published in 1918. You might be thinking that 1918 was a long time ago but a recent Hay Group survey of 450 human resource directors confirmed what Carnegie wrote almost eighty years ago: Social skills are very important to success on the job and are looked for in potential employees.

I know what some of you are thinking: There is *no way,* as an engineer, that only 15 percent of your financial success is dependent on your technical knowledge. Even if you don't believe the 85/15 split, would you at least concede that *some* of your present and *future* financial success is due to people and leadership skills? And if so, how big does it have to be for you to want to pursue that percentage? As a personal testimony, I've seen opportunity after opportunity unlocked in my professional life by focusing additional effort on becoming more skillful with people. You will get the same results if you spend more time growing yourself in this area, too.

In Daniel Goleman's book *Emotional Intelligence,* he talked about the importance of emotional intelligence, which is the ability to empathize with others, regulate one's moods, and motivate oneself in the face of frustrations, among many other traits. He stated that IQ contributes at most 20 percent to a person's overall success in life. The other 80 percent is due to factors like one's skill with people. This means that regardless of your intelligence, the majority of your success in life lies in your ability to effectively manage yourself and those around you. You've probably seen some very smart people do some incredibly stupid things.

Intelligence, it would seem, does not always equate to successful living.

This isn't about your overall success in terms of your current situation, but about your overall success throughout your entire life—your *potential*. If you're thinking only within the context of your current position, that's thinking too small. Think about where you want to be ten, fifteen, twenty years from now, and you'll quickly start to realize the importance of navigating relationships better.

You may be looking at your *current* situation and thinking you don't need people skills—they aren't that important to what you're doing right now. What you don't see is that if you had strong people skills, you might not even be *in* your current situation. You might be a co-founder of a company, a CTO of a growing business, or the technical lead of a multi-million-dollar project. You have no idea how many opportunities have passed you by. You're only aware of your current reality, which may have nothing to do with where you *could* be.

Maybe you want to start your own company. Your ability to attract and keep the best employees is going to be heavily dependent on your skill with people, and not just on your vision for the organization.

If someone else is starting a company, it could be a great opportunity for you. If you mismanaged previous relationships, you may never get the opportunity to work there because people won't want to work with you. This stuff happens all the time. People want to be around people they like. If you are more likable, you get more opportunities. It's just the way the world works.

For those of you who have reached great levels of success based solely on your technical knowledge, here's your challenge: How much more successful could you be if you also mastered the skills covered in this book? Is it possible that you think you are successful, but you haven't even scratched the surface of your potential? Potential that can only be reached by being more skillful with others? Remember, many times you aren't aware of the opportunities that pass you by when you mismanage a relationship, they simply never materialize. To reach the highest levels of success in our lives, we need to be both: skilled at our job and skilled with people.

You may have spent years and years trying to maximize your technical ability. Engineers have dozens of technical books available on the technologies they use every day as part of their normal workflow. You may keep reading books, taking courses, and practicing concepts in your free time, only to slowly climb the corporate ladder or to stay put most of the time. It may be very discouraging when it seems you are constantly surrounded by people who seem to be better than you—they have more of a natural knack for the work. So what do you do? Do you keep reading, taking more classes, and spending more and more of your time trying to maximize your technical skills? It can be exhausting, and you may not make the progress you're after. This same phenomenon may be felt in other areas of your life as well.

I've played guitar for more than twenty years. I've practiced so much that for me to get better, I literally must practice for hours and hours on whatever small new concept I'm trying to learn. It's quite possible I've almost maxed out my ability, and there are no more huge gains to be had.

People experience the same thing from a career standpoint. They dump in huge amounts of time and effort trying to maximize an area with very little return available. You may feel like you've hit a ceiling at work, and there's no place left to go from a raw technical ability standpoint. You're experiencing what is colloquially referred to as the Law of Diminishing Returns: the tendency for a continuing application of effort or skill toward a project or goal to decline in effectiveness after a certain level of result has been achieved. That's why focusing more effort on other areas of growth (the 85 percent from Carnegie's book) can be so valuable and rewarding. Instead of focusing all your time on technical ability, use your newfound knowledge to quickly maximize your *overall* potential by strengthening your people skills.

BETTER HEALTH

In addition to causing efficiency problems, strained relationships on the job also create stress, and stress *literally* kills you. Webmd.com, mayoclinic.com, and healthline.com all list similar symptoms of stress, which are as follows:

- Weakened immune system
- Heart problems
- Sadness and depression
- High blood pressure
- Stomach problems
- Anxiety
- Drug or alcohol abuse
- Sleep problems
- Fertility problems
- Arthritis

Webmd.com states 75–90 percent of all doctor's office visits are for stress-related ailments and complaints. Yikes! Our inability to properly manage our relationships at work and at home may be putting many of us in an early grave. Even if *you* can handle the stress, what about the people you work with? Are *you* contributing to the listed problems for someone else?

If you've ever experienced a stressful relationship at work, you can probably attest to the negative effects it had on your emotional and physical state. On one occasion, I experienced significant problems with a new manager. It was her first time managing, and we didn't hit it off right out of the gate. We both had a very uncomfortable six months as we tried to figure out how to make things work more smoothly. Remembering back, the problems completely dominated my thinking, and I had a hard time leaving them at the office door when I left for the day. As a result, issues at work spilled over into other areas of my life. I let the problems rent space in my brain, and I spent time outside of work fretting over a situation *at* work. It felt like I never left the office, because my thoughts were consumed with work-related problems. It was exhausting. After that experience, I've resolved to *never* let that happen again in *any* area of my life. It's just not worth it. You can do the same!

After reading this book, you'll have tools you can use to fix some of these common relational issues before they become major problems. Pick out the weed when it's small, before it has time to take root.

SUMMARY

➤ Of the five key dynamics of effective teams that Google researchers identified, psychological safety was by far the most important. In psychologically safe teams, team members feel accepted and respected.

➤ Leadership and communication skills are often taken into consideration when promoting individuals and deciding who should be paid more.

➤ The Opportunity Tree is a visual representation of how your future opportunities come through healthy connections to other individuals. More connections mean more potential opportunities.

➤ Your success as an engineer isn't dependent solely on your technical ability; it's a combination of technical prowess and skill with people. Your lack of skill with people may be putting a ceiling on your advancement as an engineer.

➤ Inability to properly manage relationships can cause stress, and stress has a significant negative impact on your overall health and quality of life. Stress literally kills people.

CHAPTER 2

Landing the Job

Picture this. Two days ago, your manager asked you to interview a candidate who appears to possess all the required skills for an open position on your team. You say yes, but secretly you are getting a little burnt-out on having to spend so much time away from your computer, the only spot where you can get any *real* work done. The interview is scheduled for 9:00 a.m., but you normally don't get into work until 10:00 a.m., which means you'll need to get up a little earlier to make sure you get to the office on time and are coherent enough to assemble your thoughts into some sort of rational order.

    The morning of the interview arrives. You drag yourself out of bed early and manage to make it to the office in enough time to chug a cup of coffee and review the applicant's résumé one last time before he arrives. On paper, he looks great. He graduated from a reputable university, has some internship experience, and even had a couple white papers published. You think: "Awesome. He's going to be a great addition to the team."

At about 9:15 a.m., the candidate rolls in and only casually apologizes for being late—something about not being able to find a parking spot. You're only mildly annoyed, because after all, *you* had to get to the office on time. In addition, on first glance, you're kind of shocked that *this* is the candidate, considering how he's dressed. He looks like he's more prepared for a Hawaiian luau then an on-site interview. He doesn't even shake your hand or ask how you're doing. "Strike one," you're thinking to yourself.

As the interview progresses, you begin to form an even more grim opinion of the fellow. For starters, he slouches in his chair when he's answering your questions, indicating he's not even that interested. He also acts like the questions are beneath him, yet never satisfactorily answers most of them. He nails the design problems, but based on his overall flippant attitude, you're unsure if he'd be an asset or detriment to the team in the long run. If he acts this way at an interview, how's he going to act every day when he comes to work?

How do you see this interview scenario playing out for the candidate? Do you think he'll get the job? Do you think there are things he could have done better to make himself more attractive to the interviewers? Of course he could have. And the same thing goes for you when you're trying to successfully navigate *your* interviews. You may not grossly violate expectations like this candidate, but take the necessary steps to make sure you're as far away from *known* bad behaviors as possible.

This chapter details specific actions that will put the odds in your favor when interviewing. How you conduct yourself can help the interviewers make decisions based on your skills, instead of getting hung up on behaviors that are fairly easy to fix and are known to raise red flags in the minds of the people who are interviewing you.

The long interview process isn't just about your technical ability. Whenever you're interviewing, either on the phone or on-site, your people skills are an important factor in propelling you to the next stage in the process. Paying attention to interpersonal details will increase your odds of being hired. You may have heard it before, but it bears repeating: If people don't like you, they won't hire you. You'll be thanked for your time, but they won't be interested.

Companies typically have you meet with more than just technical interviewers. Potentially, anyone you meet can have input as to whether you should be hired or not. Be aware of this and always be on top of your game. I've personally sat in interview wrap-up meetings where we've decided not to go with a candidate because of their personality or their inability to communicate effectively.

Some candidates are eliminated right out of the gate, and never even get a chance to interview, because they have been difficult to work with in the past. Conversely, some individuals are more aggressively pursued because of their personality and technical skills. Think of this *now* while you're working with your current team. You never know when one of your current team members will cross your path again or make an opportunity available to you in the future.

This may sound a little strange, but in a way, hiring a person is like welcoming someone into your family. You may end up working with some people for *years*. Make yourself the type of person other people want to be around, and the decision to hire you will be that much easier.

SURVIVING THE PHONE SCREEN

You submitted your résumé, caught the attention of a hiring manager or recruiter, and now they want to take it a step further. This is exciting, but can also be nerve-wracking because someone is going to call you and ask you questions about your past work experience. If you're right out of college, some recruiters will even ask you basic engineering questions to see where you are with the fundamentals. How are you supposed to prepare for that?

If you have a choice, set up the phone call at a time when you're most alert and do your best work. Ideally, the recruiter will ask what time works best for you. Use the opportunity to schedule the interview when you're in top form. You absolutely don't want to be talking to a hiring manager or recruiter when you're not at 100 percent power. Set the odds in your favor right off the bat.

How comfortable are you with the quality of your cell calls? Do they constantly break up, or worse, drop all the time? If you know you have a sketchy cell connection, find a place that has good cell phone coverage for the call, or better yet, have them call you on a landline if you have one available. Phone interviews are hard enough without having to worry about technical problems. How frustrating to get a call from your dream company, only to have the call dropped once, twice, or multiple times! Address everything you can control before the call begins, and remove some variables from the equation, if possible.

If the individual conducting the phone screen calls you, and you don't answer, that makes you look *really* bad. Be ready at least 10 minutes prior and make sure your environment is quiet and free from distractions. You don't want any background noise—you want to be able to focus all your energy on what is being said during the interview.

Familiarize yourself with the job description, research the company, and be prepared to answer questions about your résumé and past job experience. Go back over your résumé and make sure you can connect the dots between prior work and the job you are interviewing for. Saying things like "I don't really remember much about that project" aren't going to help you. Know it cold. Have a copy of your résumé and the description of the job you're applying for in front of you so you can easily tie past projects to what you think the company might be looking for.

Have pen and paper available for taking notes. You can write down the answers to your questions and record any additional questions you might have as the phone screen proceeds. Prepare a few questions to ask the interviewers if the opportunity arises. This demonstrates you are interested in the job and not just fishing for opportunities. The individuals screening you like questions because it shows you are interested in the position. Don't be afraid to ask questions—this may be where you end up spending a great deal of your time in the coming years.

When being screened or interviewed in any environment, remember your likability is also being assessed along with your technical ability. Stir yourself up and get excited! Dress like the phone call is important. Stand up. Smile. Your energy and enthusiasm will come through the phone.

Lastly, be gracious and thank your screener(s) for their time. The people who called you probably have ten other things they could be doing instead. Make sure to let them know that you genuinely appreciate the time they spent with you. This simple act will leave a positive impression of you in their mind as they hang up the phone.

PREPARING FOR THE ON-SITE INTERVIEW

I suspect most of you have experienced situations in the past where, looking back, you were embarrassed because you didn't act or speak appropriately in a particular situation. The advice in this section will go a long way toward keeping that from happening on the day of your on-site interview. For some, these suggestions may be a review of the best practices you already know. For others, it may be new material. Either way, read the guidelines and use them to get ready for one of the most critical parts of landing the job you want.

At least a week in advance, start preparing for the softer (non-technical) aspects of your interview. If you're a procrastinator, you may want to put off some of the prep work tasks until the day before your interview. Bad idea! Don't do this.

Prior to your interview, learn all you can about the company offering the position. Research who their customers are. Read all the recent news articles you can find about what's been happening lately. If it's a software company, download or sign up for a trial version of their software. If it is a hardware (HW) company, get a piece of their HW or a virtual simulator. Interviewers *love* to see passion for what their company does, both from a technology and a business perspective. This is an easy detail to shore up, so spend a little time up front making sure you can hold a semi-informed conversation about the company and their products with the interviewers.

Prepare a list of questions *you* want answered during your interview. It's important to know what you're getting into. Here is an example list to get you started:

- What are normal working hours?
- Are there any telecommuting options?
- How are performance reviews conducted?
- Are there training opportunities available?
- What does a typical work environment look like (cube, workstation, software tools, etc.)?
- Are employees on-call during various times of the month?
- What are the specifics of the vacation, insurance, and retirement plans?
- Where do employees park (if it isn't obvious)?
- Where does the company see itself in five years (its growth potential)?

Also ask about the product(s) you'll be working on, and anything else interesting you dug up from your pre-interview research. You want to know, to the best of your ability, what you're walking into if you end up accepting an offer.

Initially, your appearance is the *only* thing people judge you by, and they will make assumptions about other areas of your life based on it. It's not fair, but it's reality. As David J. Schwartz, author of *The Magic of Thinking Big,* wrote, "Your appearance is the *first* basis for evaluation other people have." You'd be surprised what kind of conclusions people will draw about you based solely on how you look. What do you want them to think about *you* when they first see you? If you want them to think you're a straight shooter with upper management written all over you, then dress that way.

The University of Missouri put this advice on their Career & Professional Development web page: "Inappropriate clothing could cost you a job, but an Armani suit isn't enough to get you a job." The goal of your attire is to convey that you think the interview is important, and you're treating it as such. Don't let your clothes be a distraction. From an interviewer's perspective, it's just another box to check concerning your interview performance.

For an interview, men may wear khakis or slacks and a long-sleeved collared shirt with or without a tie. Suits may be appropriate, but are typically overkill. Women may wear slacks and a nice blouse with or without a jacket, or a dress typical of what other successful business women in the same field might wear. Like men, a suit may be appropriate but is usually overkill. Whatever you decide, stick with the professional norms of dress. While you may not be dinged for overdressing, you will most definitely lose points for dressing like the interview was an afterthought. Avoid fashion extremes when deciding what to wear. Save your Star Wars shirts for *after* you get the job.

The most important thing to do the day before your interview is to get a good night's sleep. Trying to cram the night before instead of sleeping may negatively affect your performance in the waning hours of your interview. You want to be sharp and rested for your entire interview, not just the first couple hours. If you waited until the last minute to prepare, let the dream of successfully preparing the night before go and make sure you get enough sleep.

On the morning of the interview, have a light breakfast like a bagel, oatmeal, or fruit. If you think you'll be hungry before lunch, pack a snack (granola bar, apple, etc.) to take along. This allows you to better regulate your energy. Avoid drinking a 32-ounce latte before the interview because you don't want to have to use the restroom every five minutes. If your bladder goes into overdrive when you're nervous, this is especially important.

If you have access to a car, consider scouting out the exact interview location ahead of time, especially if you're from out-of-town. Doing this will remove some of the anxiety the morning of the interview because you'll already know the *exact* route to take to get to your interview. Instead of having to continually circle around the block or trying to decide what lane to drive in on the freeway, you'll be listening to *Eye of the Tiger,* getting yourself psyched up for the day of interviews.

TIPS FOR THE DAY OF THE ON-SITE INTERVIEW

On the day of the interview, plan to arrive at *least* twenty minutes early. This may sound crazy, but I don't know of a single instance of a candidate being passed up for being too early to an interview. Conversely, you could immediately disqualify yourself by being late. Showing up twenty minutes early leaves you plenty of time to deal with bad weather, accidents, detours, and parking issues. Do you really want road construction to cause you to be late to what might be the most exciting career opportunity of your life? You'll make a better impression being twenty minutes early than five minutes late.

In addition to how you're dressed, the expression you wear on your face can make a positive first impression. When you meet people for the first time, smile. This is one of the simplest things you can do to put the odds in your favor. Act like you're excited to be interviewed! All things being equal, people want to work with people who are happy. As Senior Software Engineer Aaron Krogh put it, "People remember funny, smiling, and engaging people differently than they do shy, mumbling, disheveled, and egotistical ones." How do you want people to remember you after your day of interviews?

When introduced to each of your interviewers, shake their hand, get their name, and say something like, "Nice to meet you, Bill." Make it a point to remember their names because you'll want to call them by name when your time with them is done. Also, if you do end up accepting a job offer, you'll use their names to thank them when you come back. If you need to, write down the names of every single person you meet during your day of interviews so you won't forget. It's *that* important.

Another small detail to a successful interview is looking people in the eyes when you speak. For some people, this is natural. For others, it is not. Eye contact varies by culture, but in Western cultures, it's considered part of proper communication. Being mousy (excessively quiet or aloof) in the interview may signal a bigger problem to the interviewers. Be confident and look at people when you're speaking to them.

During your interview, one of your primary jobs is to find out if the position is a good fit for *you*. You may be tempted to focus only on proving that you're a qualified candidate, but the company needs to demonstrate that they're a good fit for you, too. If it's the wrong job, you need to find that out *before* you accept an offer and start working. Remember that list of questions you previously prepared? Make it a point to ask all those questions and listen carefully to the answers before you leave. You'll want to make an informed decision if and when you get a job offer. Interviewers typically ask if you have any questions, so this shouldn't be an issue.

During a full day of interviews, you'll typically be treated to lunch. Use this as an opportunity to talk about topics not related to engineering, if the opportunity arises. Remember, though, that you're still being evaluated. People who join you for lunch may have been chosen specifically to assess your people skills. The meal may seem casual, but it serves as an opportunity to get a more complete picture of you as an individual. Watch what you say, because there is no downtime on a day of interviews. Save your political rants for your conversations with friends.

While at lunch, order something light and easy to eat. You want to be able to eat fast and continue talking since you're still selling yourself. If you have more interviews after lunch, you don't want a 32-ounce rib eye steak swimming around in your stomach. If your body is like mine, it may try and power down after a big meal. You don't want to deal with this while you're talking to the director of a major department.

Try to keep your energy levels as high as you can throughout the day. You may feel tired as the day drags on, but pretend that *every* person you talk to is the first person you have spoken with. Remember, *this is the first time they have ever met you.* They may ask the *exact* same questions someone else has, but you have to *make* yourself answer with the same energy and enthusiasm each time. Although this performance can be extra challenging throughout the day, don't let your excitement wane because later, all these people are going to give their input as to whether the company should extend you an offer or not.

Sometimes it becomes apparent throughout the interview process that the position isn't for you. It's OK to not want to work for a company. If you reach that decision as the interview progresses, don't let your energy level and enthusiasm wane. *Act* like you want the job more than anything else, or people will pick up on your diminished excitement and sense that you're not that interested. Remember the Opportunity Tree? The interviewers may know people in other companies who might need someone like you, so you don't want to do anything that'll leave a bad impression on them. Leave the yes or no decision until after the interview, and at the very least, count the experience as good interview practice.

In Frank Bettger's book *How I Raised Myself from Failure to Success in Selling,* he wrote, "I firmly believe enthusiasm is by far the biggest single factor in successful selling." On your day of interviews, that's exactly what you are doing—selling yourself. You need to show you're enthusiastic about the company's product line, that you love being an engineer, and that you have passion for the type of work the company does. All things being equal, a person like this has a *huge* advantage over someone with the same professional experience who talks like a monotone robot. During a day of interviews, you are a salesman. Don't let your kids go hungry because you can't sell a vacuum.

This is going to sound cliché, but after you're finished with your day of interviews, send a follow-up email to all of the interviewers. Thank them for their time and the opportunity to learn more about the company. Good manners give you additional exposure that might set you apart from other applicants. You might be surprised to know that not everyone does this simple act.

By focusing on the details of interviewing, you may not only prevent yourself from being disqualified from consideration for a position, but you can make yourself more attractive to those who ultimately have the decision-making power. Companies usually interview multiple people for the same job. If you stand out because you paid attention to the information just covered, you have a significant advantage over others with similar experience who did not. You may not be hired exclusively because of your people skills, but they definitely have a role to play in the process. If you ignore them, you're forfeiting some amount of control over the process, and that's typically never a good thing when it comes to interviewing.

SUMMARY

> Whether you're interviewing on the phone or on-site, your people skills are a big factor in propelling you to the next stage in the process.

> Get excited about your phone screen. Remove distractions from your environment, find out all you can about the company, and authentically exude passion and enthusiasm.

> One of the primary goals of an on-site interview is to find out if the job opportunity is a good fit for you. Come prepared with questions on the topics that may not be covered by the interviewers.

- ➤ Your punctuality, demeanor, and dress are all used to form an impression of you during your day of interviews.

- ➤ There is no downtime on your day of interviews. If you are taken to lunch, you are still being evaluated. Keep your energy levels high and realize you are always selling yourself. Do the simple things like smiling and looking at people in the eyes when you speak to them.

- ➤ Enthusiasm is one of the most important traits to possess when convincing someone to do or buy something. Being excited and enthusiastic with your interviewers *will* make a difference in their perception of you.

CHAPTER 3

Joining an Existing Team

Whether you've been an engineer for thirty years or this is your first job out of college, you can do certain things when joining an existing team that will ensure your transition goes smoothly and will prevent you from creating any unnecessary interpersonal problems in the process. Your primary goal as a new team member is to integrate as quickly as possible and begin contributing as fast as you can.

After joining a team, immediately get to work building the relationships necessary to succeed after your initial honeymoon period is over. Making a positive first impression and connecting with people is critical to your long-term success and happiness; as failure to do so can cause dissatisfaction, reduced efficiency, and reduced team morale. People leave companies because they fail to integrate with the existing culture or don't personally connect with their new co-workers.

When you first arrive, you'll probably start off with almost everyone being indifferent toward you. The other engineers and managers are feeling you out, formulating an opinion of you. What you do after that is up to you. People will eventually like you more or less based on what you say and do—it's completely in your control.

By practicing a handful of principles in this book, you can impress those around you and start things off on a positive note. Don't go rogue, thinking the tried-and-true principles of proper human interaction don't apply to you. That attitude only makes the difficult task of joining a team even harder. Instead, conduct yourself in a polite and respectful manner, and you won't have to guess where you stand with the rest of your team.

When joining a new team, remember that first impressions are *very* important. In fact, bad first impressions are nearly unchangeable in the minds of those who hold them. If you don't spend a lot of time around some people, and you make a bad first impression, you may not have many opportunities to change it. To make matters worse, these individuals with a bad initial impression of you could possibly end up influencing decisions about your future. How frustrating to have someone adding negative commentary to a discussion when they've only been around you for a few minutes and don't know the *real* you. Remember the branches of the Opportunity Tree and the importance of *every* interaction you have.

As discussed in the previous chapter, the way you dress can make a positive first impression. If you've joined something bigger than a start-up, most people in your new company haven't seen you yet and you'll want to make a good first impression with them, too. Dress nicely for the first week on the job, even if there is a casual dress code. You may have a closet full of anime shirts dying to be worn, but initially, it's more important to make a solid first impression with every person you meet. Typically, in the first few days, you'll meet a lot of upper management who'll want to welcome you to the company. Don't miss out on this easy opportunity to impress them.

On your first day of work, consider bringing small gifts for the people on your new team. You're typically in contact with your new manager prior to your first day so you can easily find out how many people to buy or make for. An easy idea is to buy donuts within your first couple days. Who doesn't like donuts? The goal is show how grateful and appreciative you are for being given the opportunity to work with the new team. Rather than just *think* it, *show* it as well. In many cases, being skillful with people is simply acting on many of the good practices we've already heard and observed before.

Observe and note certain dynamics at play whenever joining a new team, including but not limited to, personalities, histories between individuals, and pecking order already operating within the existing organization. For instance, each team typically has a technical lead who is the resident top nerd (not to be mistaken with the elite flight school from the 1980s movie *Top Gun*). Sometimes these people are territorial or feel like they need to reestablish their position within the group when new individuals join their team. For some engineers, their titles and positions are *extremely* important to them. While that's not necessarily a bad thing, be aware of what's going on and work *with* it instead of doing things that will trigger a territorial response from them. If you see this potential, identify these individuals early on and take steps to mitigate any problems that might otherwise cause hurt feelings or resentment on your end.

In the subdivision where I live, we are allowed to have a few laying hens. Because a large bird of prey ate one of mine, I wanted to get a couple more so my last surviving chicken, Oreo, wouldn't be all by herself. She needed some friends. When spring arrived, we found a local farmer who was selling young hens and bought two more.

When you introduce new chickens to each other, you're supposed to keep them separated so they can get acclimated to each other. Chickens have a strict hierarchy, and some of the older chickens can be aggressive toward the new ones. Based on this information, I kept them separated with chicken wire for a few weeks to make sure they were comfortable around each other before finally putting them in the same pen together.

The day finally arrived, and I decided it was time to put the new chickens in with the older one. I removed the chicken wire, then proceeded to watch our sweet Oreo stomp the other smaller chickens into the corner of the chicken pen. After seeing this, I quickly put the barrier back in place and gave them more time to get used to each other.

Some engineers are like Oreo. They will "stomp" you out and put you in your place to show you who's boss, especially if they feel their status on the team is being threatened. Their title and position are *extremely* important to them. Be aware of this possibility and avoid doing things that may stir up a territorial response. There is an entire chapter later in the book about how to correctly deal with conflict.

When just starting, stay in listen mode and respect what people are telling you, even if you think what they're doing is wrong. You'll have plenty of time later to challenge the status quo and bring about change. In the beginning, gather as much information as you can about your new team and the business without rocking the boat. No one likes being told they are wrong by someone who just started working four hours ago, even if they *are* wrong. You don't want to get stomped into the corner by challenging the established pecking order prematurely. Get to know your new teammates first and show that you're not a threat to anyone or the existing process that's in place. You're there to help. In a later chapter, you'll find tips about how to tell people they're wrong, if and when that time comes.

If you're hired into a new company in a technical leadership position, it's extremely important to know how to initially approach your new team. If you come in with an "I'm the new top dog, and here's how we're changing things" approach, prepare for resistance and strife. After all, people don't know you, what you stand for, and are unsure of your motives. Some people on your team may have interviewed for the job you now hold. How do you think they feel about that?

Before you try to lead people, spend time connecting with them. Doing so will go a long way in easing any possible tensions and will demonstrate that you aren't a direct threat to them. In John Maxwell's book *The 21 Irrefutable Laws of Leadership,* he put it this way: "The stronger the relationship and connection between individuals, the more likely the follower will want to help the leader." If you're a new leader, you need all the help you can get, which means you'll want to connect with people before making any sweeping organizational changes. This strategy may seem like a waste of time, but it's not. This subject is discussed in more detail in the chapter titled "Leading Technical Teams."

To integrate smoothly with your new team, find out what the normal work schedule is, and then add a little extra time on each side of it. For example, if most engineers work 9:00 a.m. to 5:00 p.m., consider working 8:30 a.m. to 5:30 p.m. Be in the office when most people roll in and stay until most people roll out. The little extra time lets people know that you're a hard worker. Again, all you're doing is demonstrating your existing work ethic and dedication. Your goal is to make a solid first impression. As you work at your new company longer, you can adjust your schedule to what works best for you.

Being a new member of a team can be frustrating because you want to help, but you typically don't have the expertise or experience to immediately contribute. You may jokingly feel like your only way to add any sort of value is to get coffee or snacks for the current engineers doing *real* work. Even if you are a seasoned engineer, there is an expected ramp-up time when joining a new team because every company (and team) seems to design, deliver, and support their products in a unique way. Understanding this complexity is hard and takes a while.

Balance self-help with seeking guidance from others by attempting to figure out things for yourself before asking for help from your co-workers. This will give you a deeper understanding of whatever problem you're trying to solve without over-burdening people on your new team with questions you don't really need to ask in the first place. If you *can't* find a solution by yourself, don't be afraid to ask for help. There is a balance here. Be aware of how much time you're spending on an issue and ask for help after you've put in a reasonable amount of effort.

As of the writing of this book (2018), it's a *very* good time to be an engineer. The pay is great, the work is interesting, and the projected growth in most engineering fields is "up and to the right." Because of the competitive marketplace for our skill sets, we may easily slip into an entitlement mindset where we think things are owed to us, and we can ignore many of the standard best practices concerning interpersonal interactions. Following the unwritten rules of conduct when joining a new team can prevent unnecessary problems later. For instance, Nerd Street Cred (NSC) is a very real thing. We get NSC by being dependable, helpful, and continually showing that we can get our work done on time with a high degree of quality. With NSC comes certain perks like flexible hours and telecommuting. Your new company may offer these to every employee, but have you *earned* them? Don't attempt to work from Starbucks on your second day when everyone knows that you have no idea what you're doing. That's an extreme example, but it conveys the point: Build up your NSC and people, including management, won't question some of the liberties you decide to take later on.

When someone helps you (and you'll need a *lot* of help at first), take time to thank them. If they go above and beyond by spending a significant amount of time and effort to help you, show your appreciation in a tangible way when it's appropriate. Take them to coffee or find out what their favorite snack or drink is and leave it on their desk with a short note thanking them for taking the time to help you. The average person feels habitually underappreciated, and you can use opportunities like this to stand out from everyone else. As a result, you may be surprised at how helpful these people can be in the future.

Spending time with your team members is one of the best ways to get to know them. What do they like to do outside of work? What interesting technical projects are they working on in their spare time? Connecting with people on a personal level will spill over into the workplace in a positive way. When people know you and like you, they will typically be more amiable to helping you, even when it's inconvenient for them. They are helping an acquaintance, not a stranger. How motived are *you* to help someone that you don't know or like versus a friend or associate?

Let other people find out that you're a good person by giving them the opportunity to get to know you. Most of us spend at least as much time with our co-workers as we do with our families. Since we're together so much of the time, we may as well enjoy being around each other as much as possible.

Remember, to make a good impression, you must do things that impress people. This doesn't mean engaging in over-the-top antics, but simply doing the small things that everyone likes to see in a dependable, hard-working individual. Take advantage of human nature and do the things that leave a good taste in people's mouths. These actions will start you off the right way and short-circuit much bigger problems that will now be completely avoided altogether.

SUMMARY

➤ Certain dynamics are present on a team when a new engineer comes on board. Being aware of them allows you to sidestep many potential problems.

➤ Do the things that will make a good first impression on your new team members.

➤ Listening is one of your primary roles when joining a new team. Challenging team deliverables and direction prematurely can cause unnecessary relational friction.

- Appreciate people in a tangible way if their help warrants it.

- Spend time getting to know each of your new team members. It's kind of like greasing the gears before turning on a big machine.

- If you want to impress other engineers, do things that are impressive—not only from a technical standpoint, but from a people skills perspective as well.

CHAPTER 4

Dealing with Management

In Gallup's 2015 study, *The State of the American Manager,* they found that 50 percent of working Americans have left a job to "get away from their manager at some point in their career." While the specifics of those separations were not provided, lack of basic people skills was likely a contributing factor in the employee's decision to leave. Is that too big of a leap in logic? Not really. It's similar to saying "sheep go where the grass is." When the grass dries up, the sheep move on because that's what sheep do. When employees feel underappreciated, disrespected, and marginalized, they naturally move on to where the "grass" appears to be greener, too. It's basic human nature.

You have a significant role to play in the quality of your relationship with your manager. If you like where you work, you should do everything in your power to make sure the relationship is healthy, because failing to do so could be the beginning of the end with your current employer. What a shame to have a job you enjoy, but ultimately feel like you have to leave because you ignored basic interpersonal best practices. With a reported 50 percent of people leaving their jobs because of their managers, it happens all the time, even in fields that typically have more educated management who received formal training and should know better.

It's easy to point fingers at the other person and blame them for the state of the relationship, but typically relationships deteriorate because *both* parties are not behaving correctly. Managers should be well versed in the material covered in this book, but relationships are like dancing: It's a team effort in which both participants need to know the proper steps for it to work correctly. You are an active participant in this relationship dance, not a bystander. If you do things right on your end, at the very least, you won't make the situation worse. If neither party is doing their part correctly, it's guaranteed to fail. Behave like a mature professional, and then use any available opportunities to influence the other person. Other forms of dealing with problems, such as engaging in passive-aggressive behavior, are doomed to failure.

GETTING ALONG WITH YOUR MANAGER

This may come as a shocker, but some managers need people skills more than you do. You might have to be the adult in your interactions with them until the situation changes. Avoid making the problem worse by choosing to treat them, and possibly others, in the same immature way you are currently being treated. Mimicking poor behavior out of frustration is not a solution to the problem. Conversely, you may be surprised at how quickly bad situations can turn around when you start using techniques known to elicit the right kind of behaviors from others.

If you were to ask my co-workers about me, I think most would say that I'm easy to get along with and fun to be around. At least I *hope* that's what they'd say. After years of working on my people skills, I'm to the point where I feel like I'm able to quickly connect with others and avoid unproductive interpersonal problems. With all that said, there are certain personalities that are *still* very hard for me to deal with. Some people seem to zig when I zag. Conversations are weird, and we seem to read each other's intentions incorrectly. It's like I'm talking to someone from another planet. I bet there are people in your life that for some reason are hard for you to connect with, too. I had a manager that fell into this category at one point in my career, which made interactions even more strained than they should have been.

When you run into these types of people, you have two choices:

1. Avoid them as much as you can because of how odd the interactions feel.
2. Look for opportunities to work through the oddness by applying principles covered in this book and take control of the situation so you have more direct control on the outcome.

You could throw your hands in the air, convince yourself that you're the victim, and give up before you've tried to address the problems, but that doesn't do anything to solve the current issues you're facing. If every person you encountered was easy to get along with, there would be no reason for all the existing relationship training (leadership, marriage, etc.). Fortunately, or unfortunately, there are plenty of people to practice on.

Believe it or not, your manager is there to help you. Managers want you to succeed because when you succeed, they succeed, too. This is the devil's bargain of being a manager: Their success depends on how successful their teams are. If a team flops, the manager flops. You may not feel like your manager is on your side because they are also tasked with the unenviable job of giving candid performance feedback to you and your team. However, most managers don't actively try to sabotage the people they manage because they don't want to sabotage their own success. If you've worked for a manager who actively undermined individuals on the team, that behavior is not the norm, so don't lump all managers in with that unpleasant experience.

Managers have interesting roles and responsibilities within a company. They must balance the needs of the company with the needs of the people on their teams. Sometimes they must make decisions that seem to favor the company, and sometimes they make decisions that seem to favor the employees. It's a constant back-and-forth; trying to do their best to keep the troops happy *and* deliver on company objectives. Because of this line they walk, many controversial decisions a manager makes are nothing more than the manager having to pick the company over the employee in a specific situation. This happens occasionally, and you don't want to misconstrue this action as some sort of personal attack on you. It's the role they are paid to play. Alternatively, when wearing the other hat, managers will push *back* against company directives and fight for what's best for their direct reports. It's not an easy job.

If you make things difficult for your manager, it's probably going to come back on you. Managers are people, too (gasp!), and they want to avoid problems at work just as much as you do. Whatever you can do to make their lives easier will go a long way in making your life easier as well. If you're condescending, short, and combative during interactions with your manager, don't be surprised when that's exactly what you get in return. You never want to be accused of treating your manager the exact opposite of the way you want to be treated. That's what a hypocrite would do.

For example, I knew a manager that was charged with handpicking engineers for a new team that was tasked with mapping out and pursuing some exciting new objectives for the company. After managing the team for a short period of time, he abruptly announced he was leaving and took another position elsewhere within the company. The members of his team were completely caught off guard by the announcement. Later he admitted the real reason he left was because of interpersonal problems. An individual on his team caused all sorts of problems, and it was more than he could handle. He decided it was better to leave the exciting opportunity than to stay in a bad work environment. What is the point of this story? Problems between individuals are hard on everyone. The team lost a good manager, and the man prematurely left a great position all because of one individual. Managers feel the stress of people problems as keenly as anyone else and may do much worse than simply leave the team.

You'll have few problems with *most* managers if you deliver your requirements on time, keep your managers informed of any issues (show-stopping defects, schedule slips, etc.), and employ the people skills found in this book. If you practice these skills, you will be easier to manage and your time with your manager will be uneventful in a good and productive way. Operating this way will make most managers adopt-and-go from our standpoint—they'll take over management of the team and then begin doing typical management tasks without having to fight through any significant relational issues that can be a source of stress for everyone involved.

Better relations with management can be facilitated by accepting that some managers simply don't care about the details. That's what *you* get paid to do. Not every manager has a deep technical background. Even if they wanted to hear the specifics, they wouldn't understand them. Some managers moved into management to *escape* the details because they are better at managing resources than doing engineering work. As an engineer, your life may be completely consumed with technical minutia, and you sometimes find it hard to understand why anyone *wouldn't* want to know the gory details.

Being a good engineer means gauging the technical level of your manager and giving them enough details for them to properly understand and manage your area. Take personal ownership of helping your manager understand as many of the technical details as possible without confusing them. With some managers, you may have to explain things as if you're talking to your mom, but that's OK. This is self-serving in nature because the more educated your manager is about your work, the better they can represent your efforts to others in the management chain. Confusing them won't help anyone.

You may have regularly scheduled one-on-one meetings with your manager. These meetings typically cover work-related topics, but they can also be used as opportunities to get to know your manager better on a personal level. If time allows, ask for advice about other things you're doing, what books they're reading or have read, or use this time to discuss hobbies and personal interests. Over time, your interactions with your manager will become more pleasant instead of cold, weird, and tainted with the boss–to-subordinate feel.

IF YOU WANT TO IMPRESS YOUR MANAGER, DO THESE THINGS

Companies operate in different ways. Some have annual performance reviews, some don't. Some companies rank engineers against each other, some rank them based on how they performed against stated objectives for the year. Some companies have no managers at all, although they are definitely in the minority.

In most technical companies, your manager has a significant impact on the rewards and recognition you may receive. Knowing this, you should focus some time and energy on making sure the individual with the biggest impact on your rewards (e.g., pay, bonuses, stock, and promotions) is impressed with your performance. That's not to suggest that you should become a brownnoser, only that you should exhibit the traits of an engineer that are worth rewarding.

One of the easiest and most obvious ways to impress your manager is to consistently produce high-quality deliverables on time. That may seem obvious, but it must be included here for completeness. If you develop a reputation for delivering on time and with high quality, many issues between you and management will never materialize. Management will have no reason to give you negative feedback concerning your performance, which can be the start of many interpersonal problems. If your work meets or exceeds the standards of your organization, you easily sidestep many of the problems you *could* have with management. If you struggle with the quality of your work, find a more successful engineer who can mentor you and share advice on habits that make them so effective. Doing so can quickly get your work back on track and get you back in good graces with your manager.

Taking personal responsibility for your failings and not blaming others when *you* mess up is an impressive character trait for an engineer. As R&D Director Jen Belt put it: "No engineer is perfect. Failure will happen. Proactively communicating failure and owning it will go a long way toward your credibility." When, not if, you mess up, own it. That's what mature professionals do. Communicate exactly what happened and how you're going to keep it from happening again. Managers respect this approach because it shows honesty, self-awareness, and accountability. Don't try to make excuses or blame others because those actions make *you* look bad. Being wrong can sting a little, but it's part of growing and getting better as engineers. A simple "I messed up, but I know why, and I know how to keep it from happening again" can be an impressive statement. Managers aren't looking for perfection; they are looking for predictability and continued refinement. Learning from your mistakes increases both. Hiding mistakes or blaming others is a bad character trait that may prevent you from receiving future pay raises and promotions.

You should always be honest and forthcoming with information, even if it means you look like you dropped the ball. People respect honesty. Being transparent allows managers to manage based on correct, up-to-date information. No manager likes to be surprised at the last minute with competing priorities or new work estimates. Unless you say otherwise, your manager will assume all your deliverables are on track. The only way they'll know something has slipped is if you tell them. The longer you wait to inform them about a problem, the worse you look. In general, it's best to inform management *as soon as* you think there may be an issue, even if it turns out to be a false alarm. This allows them plenty of time to put a contingency plan in place. Engaging early is always preferable to engaging late. If you show up in their office the day before a deadline and tell them you can't get a piece of work finished, they have no time to react. As one of my past managers Tommy Mouser put it, "The only thing worse than bad news, is bad news late."

When you're assigned tasks, it's your responsibility, not your manager's, to proactively drive the work. Managers are impressed when they give you a difficult task, and you do whatever is necessary to drive the task to completion. This may include scheduling your own meetings, working with teams outside your immediate area, and having your Quality Assurance (Q&A) department sufficiently test your work. You never want to sit on a deliverable and wait to be told what to do because that fosters a culture of micromanagement, something nearly every employee says they don't want. To avoid being micromanaged, prove you don't need to be micromanaged. Taking personal ownership of tasks that have been assigned to you will give your manager more to commend you on at your next performance review.

Managers like to see their engineers willing to try new things and learn new technologies. Speaking from a software perspective, new technologies are constantly being introduced into the marketplace. If you're unwilling to investigate and experiment with them, your technical skills may become antiquated. Additionally, your team may be less efficient and costlier to operate because you're not taking advantage of new tools and processes that didn't exist a few short years before. While I'm not recommending your team live on the technological edge and seriously consider adopting every new process or technology that pops up in your space, you should do a survey every so often to see what's out there and if it can help.

Some companies are willing to try and use different technologies more than others. That experimentation may be why some companies are so successful at what they do. Operating like this is contingent on you knowing what the current and new technologies are, and how they might be applied to your existing business. Staying current means that you constantly read, evaluate new offerings, and figure out how they may make your teams faster, more scalable, and more cost-effective.

This is the responsibility of every engineer, not just the senior technical leadership.

As an engineer, your permanent curiosity about different technologies can impress management because it shows you are continually trying to grow intellectually, which translates to better technical decisions for the team. Learning new technologies can be tough, but also very rewarding; some of these new technologies may save you and your company a lot of time, effort, and money. Never shy away from learning because when you stop learning, you are essentially locked into a particular space. You're frozen in time while everyone else passes you by. Software Engineer Paul Painter said it perfectly, "This (software) is a great field to work in if you don't mind taking everything you know and blowing it up every three years." Technology moves fast, and if you want to stay on top of it, you must be willing to learn and try new things.

During performance evaluations, you may receive negative feedback about your work and work habits. It can sting a little. It's tough to listen to how you're not meeting the mark in certain areas, but sometimes negative feedback is exactly what you need to hear. Respond to the feedback by internalizing it and making the necessary changes to improve your work habits going forward. Be mature enough to see through the initial discomfort of negative feedback and recognize it for what it is: an opportunity to get better. If, and when, your manager informs you of an area needing work, take it as a personal challenge to get better in that specific area. When you improve, management will be impressed. What you *don't* want to do is keep having the same difficult conversations about the same problems repeatedly. If you're unwilling to change, you're showing unwillingness to progress in your career. That will have a negative impact on your performance reviews and ultimately, the rewards you receive.

If your managers were to ask you whether you have affected your team's morale in a positive or negative way, what would you say? If they asked your team about you, what would *they* say about you? Team morale is important to your managers, and if you want to impress them in this area, avoid habitually complaining about decisions that have been made or the future direction of the team. If you have better ideas, great! Get them out on the table in a tactful manner at the appropriate time. *Consistently* pointing out why things *might* not work does nothing more than suck the life out of everyone who listens to it. Rich Payne, an engineering manager, said: "I don't like working with 'hand grenade throwers.' By this, I mean the guy that makes his living pointing out flaws or risks, particularly in the work of others. They point out weaknesses, but never really fix anything, or even propose alternatives that will work." Constant complaining is a drain on team morale and is difficult to work with. Complainers stifle team creativity because other engineers on the team will start withholding ideas due to the constant flood of negative comments received. Instead of suppressing creativity, impress management by creating a safe environment by encouraging others to share their ideas.

No matter how well you get along with others, you may still have to work with certain personalities that are very hard for you to deal with. With some managers, conversations may always be weird; you read each other's intentions incorrectly, and you feel like you're talking to someone with a completely foreign personality. Your relationship with your current manager may be more strained than it should be, but with the right people skills, it can most definitely be improved upon. Don't give up. There is hope!

Throughout your career, you will meet many types of people, and you're not going to get along with all of them. When you run into these people, decide up front that you aren't going to quit before genuinely trying to address any problems. Sometimes doing the right thing is the hardest thing you can do. Times like these are when you get to put all your interpersonal training to the test.

We don't live in a fantasy land where all our problems can be solved by simply hugging long enough and singing folk songs on an acoustic guitar. Even though the state of your relationship with your manager depends as much on them as it does on you, your manager may not be interested in behaving properly and may refuse to change. What then? If you have irreconcilable differences after *honestly* trying to make it work, you may have no other choice than to ask to be moved to a different team. Avoid the "I don't like you, I want to be moved" approach and other such confrontational methods, since that's equivalent to throwing more fuel on the already burning fire. If possible, identify another team working on a technology that interests you and ask if you can move to pursue it. Do not fight or argue with your existing manager; if you do, it will come back to haunt you. Always take the high road, even when it's tough, because people are always watching how you conduct yourself. If you handle something like this well, others will hear about it, and it may improve future opportunities.

For managers who are reading this, unless there are extraordinary circumstances at play, an employee will stay in a toxic work environment for only so long before leaving to find something better. Why would engineers waste the mental and emotional energy working for difficult managers when their skills are in such high demand all over the world? Engineers' skill sets are aggressively pursued by many companies with R&D departments, and it appears the competition for good engineers will continue into the foreseeable future. If you abuse the sheep, they will leave to find greener grass.

SUMMARY

➤ Relationships typically deteriorate because *both* parties are behaving incorrectly. Are your actions making things better or worse?

- If you make things difficult for your manager, it will probably come back on you. Managers are people, too, and don't want to deal with interpersonal friction.

- Your manager has the biggest impact on what rewards and recognition you receive throughout the year. Ignoring the traits they use to assess your performance is the same as giving them reasons *not* to give you more money, promotions, and recognition.

- If you want to impress your manager, conduct yourself in an impressive way. Deliver products on time that are high quality. Own your mistakes, contribute to positive team morale, and internalize feedback to improve your performance.

CHAPTER 5

Dealing with Difficult Engineers

If you've never had to deal with a truly difficult engineer, count yourself lucky. Many have worked with someone who is extremely talented, but very rough around the edges when it comes to interacting with other people. They are allowed to stick around because of their technical ability, but harnessing that ability comes at a price that must be paid in the form of anxiety, stress, and avoidance. If you don't come up with a plan to deal with this type of individual, your job satisfaction and overall happiness might be significantly lower than they would otherwise be. This chapter will give you some pointers on how to more effectively deal with these difficult engineers.

Before digging in too deep, here is the bad news first: Some engineers are arrogant, condescending, and self-centered, and they will *never* change. It's a sobering thought, but you're likely not naïve enough to think that every person can be changed based solely on how you conduct yourself. It's their choice to change or not; consequently, the onus is on *you* to prevent their immaturity from negatively affecting your career and happiness. Even if the difficult engineer never changes, you can avoid making the problem worse by doing your part correctly and not treating others the same way this difficult engineer is treating you. In effect, you keep the dysfunction from spreading, and that is most definitely worth pursuing.

If someone is being perpetually difficult to work with, there can be a temptation to want to avoid this person as much as possible. This seems to be the natural reaction to someone who is confrontational, unsupportive, and maybe even outright verbally abusive. The problem is, avoidance is counterproductive to getting work done, especially if this individual possesses the expertise you need to deliver on some of your commitments. What are you supposed to do, then? You can modify an old saying to, "Talented, difficult engineers: We can't live with them, and we can't live without them." You don't want to spend the rest of your life compiling a list of people to avoid because you can't handle their difficult personalities. People might end up thinking *you're* the one with a problem at that point.

Instead of continually avoiding difficult engineers or employing passive-aggressive tactics to get some sort of revenge, try exercising strategies outlined in this book that are known to reduce interpersonal strife. When dealing with people, getting better results is no more complicated than doing the right thing in each and every interaction. That's easier said than done, but you don't want to engage in behaviors proven ineffective simply because they make you feel better in the short term. Feelings are fleeting and unreliable and shouldn't be used as your guide, *especially* when you're angry or feeling slighted in some way.

ARE YOU A DIFFICULT ENGINEER?

Before compiling a mental list of all the difficult engineers you work with, first ask yourself this question: Am I a difficult engineer? Humans typically have a blind spot when it comes to our own shortcomings, so before you point your finger at others, make sure you're not conducting yourself in the same way you're accusing others of operating.

Here's a short list of ways you can tell if you're a difficult engineer:

1. Your manager tells you to work on your communication skills.

This is the most obvious indicator. If your manager ever tells you this, what she's really saying is, "I've had complaints from other employees that you are hard to work with." Sure, it stings a little to hear it, but at least you're now aware, or are reminded, of the problem and can take the necessary steps to fix it. Your manager will probably help you get the additional training you need with regards to your people skills. You can even tell her that you're reading this book!

2. People problems follow *you* around.

If people problems follow you around wherever you go, *you* might be the problem, not the other engineers. If you experience constant relational friction at work, it might not be because everyone else needs to change—you're the one who may need to change.

3. People seem nervous around you.

If people walk on eggshells around you, seem nervous, or drastically change their personality (for example, are normally funny and outgoing, but around you are quiet and serious), it may be because they're afraid of your wrath or scathing comments. Check this gauge periodically, just like you check the gas gauge in your car. If people feel uneasy around you, take specific steps to remedy that, regardless of the cause. We'll go over additional ways to connect with others in the chapter titled "Get to Know Others."

4. You constantly challenge everything everyone says and does.

No one is ever right. Only you know how things should work. You think management always makes the wrong decisions, and the company is headed in the wrong direction. If you challenge nearly every single decision made, you may be a difficult engineer. Sure, part of your job may be designing solutions to difficult problems the company faces, but if you find yourself constantly at odds with every idea under consideration, you're probably out of balance. It's possible you have a combative personality, which isn't winning you any points with those around you. Other engineers may literally dread having to work alongside you.

5. You expect people to deal with your shortcomings.

This problem is actually quite common. You may find it hard to fix some of your shortcomings with regards to your people skills, so you've given up trying. You've decided everyone else must accept you for the way you are, instead of taking responsibility for your actions and changing them. That's the textbook definition of self-centeredness. Why should everyone else have to change just for you? You should start employing a common set of skills that will fix the problem at its source—you.

6. When people stop by to ask you questions, you view them as annoyances and distractions.

People can tell when you don't want to talk to them. If you keep your hands on the keyboard and continue to face your monitor when people stop in to ask you a question (fig. 2), the message you're giving them is: "I'm busy. I don't want to talk to you so let's get this over as soon as we can." That may be how you feel, but as we've already discussed, we don't operate on feelings. Instead, we do what's right because we want the results of doing things correctly. If people perceive that you are annoyed with them, they'll think twice before asking you questions in the future, which can have a direct impact on organizational effectiveness.

Figure 2

7. You think you're better or more important than other people because of your technical ability.

People can tell if you think too highly of yourself: Your words and actions give you away. If you think you're better or more important than other engineers because of your technical ability, it has a negative impact on your effectiveness within your team and organization. Pride, quite frankly, is one of the fastest ways to cause problems between people and is remarkably simple to avoid.

If you exhibit any or all of these seven traits, but you're not sure how big the problem might be, ask someone how others view you. If you trust a co-worker, pull them aside and ask if you're difficult to interact with. Tell them you want to improve your interactions, but you're not sure how big the problem is. To aid in the conversation, use the seven indicators to get the conversation going. When your problem areas are revealed to you, you'll be able to put some focused effort into fixing them.

ESTABLISH A RAPPORT

Some engineers may possess a sort of Dr. Jekyll and Mr. Hyde personality when it comes to work. In the office, they may be extremely difficult, but in almost every other area of their lives, they might be pleasant and laid back. To get additional perspective on them, create opportunities to connect on subjects not directly related to work. Engineers who are awkward or gruff on first encounter may be quite pleasant after you get to know them. Like a nut, you have to crack their hard, exterior shell to get to their soft, tasty center. They could be judged as difficult based solely on a thin slice of their life (work), but the perception isn't a completely accurate picture of them as a person.

I have been playing and writing music for over two decades. To be honest, it's probably the one thing in life I'm most passionate about. When playing with other musicians, I have been accused of being a taskmaster and perfectionist, which is almost laughable if you knew how I conducted myself in other areas of my life. It's easy for me to expect more from those around me than I should because music is so important to me, and I love all the little details of songwriting. If someone were to give their opinion of me based solely on being in a band with me, that opinion would be *completely* different from what others who have never interacted with me in that capacity would say about me. This very same thing can happen to engineers.

On the surface, difficult engineers may seem cold and aloof, but they may actually be nice, funny, and interesting people—you have to expend a little extra effort penetrating their shell. Have you ever met a person whom, on first impression, you didn't particularly care for but later you ended up being friends? I have. What was the breakthrough in that relationship? We spent time together, getting to know each other, and that brought balance to the relationship.

One of the simplest ways to get to know difficult engineers is to physically remove them from the setting where they're being difficult. Get them out of one headspace and into another. Buy them coffee, go for a walk together, or invite them over for dinner. These are all very effective ways to get a more complete view of a person. Since they are physically disconnected from the workplace environment, other topics of discussion will naturally arise. The new setting allows people to let their hair down a bit and discover that you aren't a threat to them and that you're a genuinely good person. Doing something as simple as grabbing a cup of coffee together can go a *long* way in building up more mutual trust.

Asking a difficult engineer to mentor you in their area of expertise is another effective approach to establishing a better working relationship. If they are very good at using a certain piece of software, ask for help in learning it. If they are really good at teasing requirements out of high-level technical deliverables, ask if they can walk you through their approach to breaking down complicated deliverables. Doing things like this gets you past that wall and allows you see things from their perspective, which ultimately allows you to relate to them better.

LEARN THEIR COMMUNICATION STYLE

Getting a better feel for a person's style of communication also helps you deal with difficult engineers. After working around someone for a while, you'll typically get a feel for how the person likes to communicate. This understanding helps you smooth out future interactions. Perhaps the difficult engineer likes to interrupt a lot. If so, be ready for it. Maybe they have an aggressive way of talking that sounds like they are constantly attacking others, even though that's not their intent. Prepare for it. The point here is to come up with a plan for increasing the odds of a successful interaction by taking the person's stated or unstated preferences and habits into account. Ideally, the difficult engineer will eventually change his counterproductive behaviors, but don't expect overnight miracles. Stick to your plan to keep your interactions positive and productive.

As you get to know the engineer better, you can initiate interactions with them using the methods they respond to best. For instance, maybe certain individuals are unhelpful and terse via email or instant-messaging (IM), but are pleasant in face-to-face interactions. Knowing this, you can approach them on *their* terms to increase the likelihood of a successful exchange and minimize interpersonal conflict. If you know someone rarely checks their IMs, don't keep trying to engage in any sort of timely conversation with them using that communication method. Go see them face-to-face instead.

When a co-worker at my company was first hired, he flat-out told everyone he wasn't going to use IM, period. He thought it was too disruptive, having had a bad experience with that communication tool when working for his previous employer. He was up-front about it, so no one contacted him via IM. This is sort of an extreme example, but most every engineer is the same way: They all have preferred forms of communication, and if you want to connect with them, be aware of their biases and use what works best for *them*. Don't get upset if someone never responds to your emails. Ask them what communication method they prefer. They'll be happy to let you know, and you can use that method instead.

SOMETIMES YOU HAVE TO GIVE IN

Sometimes when interacting with other engineers, you may have to give a little to get a little. American industrialist Jean Paul Getty quoted his father as saying: "You must never try to make all the money that's in a deal. Let the other fellow make some money too, because if you have a reputation for always making all the money, you won't have many deals." If you have a reputation for always having to have things your way, you probably have a reputation for being difficult to work with. Over the course of your career, it's more important to keep the goodwill of your co-workers than to always get what you want in every technical discussion. Some things are most definitely worth fighting for, but not everything falls into that category *all the time*. Smart engineers know when to fight and when to give in.

Some engineers like to challenge *everything*. To them, every interaction is like a power struggle. While a challenge isn't necessarily bad in certain situations, it should be tempered with thought on how the challenge affects the other team members. To gain interpersonal capital with these types of people later down the road, you may have to give in to their desires sometimes. James Penick, a Senior Software Engineer, wisely put it this way: "One strategy that I use is to occasionally give the difficult engineer what they want when it's an issue that's not particularly important to me. My hope is that, by doing this, I'll be able to demonstrate that I'm a reasonable person who is willing to give and take and that I'll have something in the 'bank' when it's something that is important to me." James recognized there's a bigger game at play in larger teams. It's not only about winning in the right now but sustained winning as a *group*.

Unfortunately, some engineers are completely blind to the side effects of their combative personalities and are bent on winning every discussion. If you work with someone like this, choose your battles wisely, or you'll end up being sucked into a counterproductive death spiral where every discussion with this individual becomes more about winning than doing what's right.

KEEP DIFFICULT PEOPLE OUT OF YOUR ORGANIZATION IN THE FIRST PLACE

This is probably obvious, but the simplest way to deal with difficult engineers is to keep them out of your organization in the first place. Don't hire them. If you don't hire difficult engineers, you won't have to spend time and energy figuring out how to work around their shortcomings. People problems are a distraction and drain energy that could be used for other more productive purposes. Instead, hiring the right engineers will let you spend those resources meeting your deadlines and delivering work that meets or exceeds your quality objectives.

In his book *Good to Great,* Jim Collins explored this topic in his chapter titled "First Who...Then What." One of the points he makes in this chapter is that, "Good-to-great leaders began the transformation (of their company) by first getting the right people on the bus (and the wrong people off the bus) and then figured out where to drive it." He states that having the right people on your team is far more important than knowing exactly what you want to do. If you have the right people, they will figure out how to get where they need to go. The key point of the chapter was that "who" questions should come before "what" decisions.

The common practice many technical companies employ is to first identify what needs to be done and *then* staff-up for the work. They'll try to get the most qualified people when they're looking, but hiring is typically done in spurts and conducted as if the openings can be revoked at any time, which is a legitimate concern in some companies. With this approach, some people are hired when they shouldn't have been. Because of time constraints placed on hiring managers, they feel like they must hire people as fast as possible due to shifting budgets, business outlooks, and project schedules. This method significantly lowers the bar for hiring, which may result in difficult engineers joining our teams, who otherwise should wait for a position that's a better fit for them.

Because engineers are in such high demand in certain markets, hiring managers tend to hire people too quickly because of a perceived talent shortage. Word of warning: This is lowering the bar for hiring. Do you want warm bodies, or do you want engineers that are technically capable, a good fit for your existing workplace culture, *and* won't cause people problems while you're trying to achieve your goals? Are you focused on hiring for the long term, or on getting an extra set of hands to help with critical deliverables in the short term? Remember, the newly hired engineers may end up working with your existing team members for *years.*

As an engineer, you have a part to play in whether people should be hired or not. When you're interviewing engineers for open positions, put emphasis on teasing out all their abilities, not just their technical ones. Always give honest feedback on their interview performance. If you think they could be a potential problem down the road, share the information with the hiring manager. You have an obligation to flag difficult people because failing to do so makes things harder for everyone later on. As Jim Collins put it: "When in doubt, don't hire. Keep looking."

Knowingly hiring people with a difficult track record is akin to putting a little bit of poison in the food you're preparing. The people eating the food may not notice the effects of the poison immediately, but over time, it starts affecting them adversely. The more poison (difficult engineers) added to the recipe (your team), the worse the problem gets. If you hire people strictly based on talent, you run the very real risk of slowly poisoning your teams to death. Consciously introducing difficult engineers into your teams in hopes that their technical abilities will make up for their lack of people skills is not a strategy for success.

SUMMARY

> Some engineers are arrogant, condescending, and self-centered, and they will *never* change. The responsibility falls to you to make up the difference.

> Are you a difficult engineer?

> Try to get the difficult engineer out of the workplace and into a different environment. Some

engineers are completely different when not doing engineering work, and this can give you a more healthy perspective of them as a person.

➤ How does the difficult engineer communicate? If they are rough around the edges, prepare for it. Sometimes people can be completely oblivious to the effects of their actions on others.

➤ Embrace the communication preferences of the difficult engineer. If they never respond to email, stop expecting timely responses or responses at all.

➤ Don't fan the flames by being difficult yourself. Sometimes you have to give a little to get a little.

➤ When in doubt, don't hire an engineer who's suspected of being difficult. It's akin to slowly poisoning your existing team.

CHAPTER 6

Leading Technical Teams

As you progress through your technical career, you naturally gain more knowledge, experience, and ultimately influence within your organization. If you solve all the difficult technical problems thrown your way, you'll establish a reputation as a top performer on your team, and people will look to you more often for input. You now have a choice to make. Squander this influence by violating the principles of effective communication and leadership, or use it to your team's advantage to remove roadblocks, iron out personality differences, and make people feel valued and appreciated. Being a successful team leader requires a larger set of people skills than it took to become a successful engineer.

In large part, successfully leading other people is dependent on your character and people skills, which you may not have used much when you were a rank-and-file engineer. Unlike computers, people have biases, prejudices, and diverse histories, which can make for a challenging work environment. Your job as a technical leader is to not only design and implement solutions to technical problems, but also to manage interpersonal dynamics between people and teams by addressing potential problems before they can affect the schedule and quality of your projects.

You might be thinking, "But that's why we have a manager—to take care of all the personnel issues." In one regard, you're right. One of the primary responsibilities of a people-manager is to address any interpersonal issues present within your team. However, once you've been promoted (formally or informally) to a higher position, it's now your responsibility to be the manager's representative when they aren't around. You've taken on some management work as a result of gaining more influence in your organization. These added responsibilities aren't necessarily a bad thing; they are simply part of moving up the technical ladder. The higher you go, the more important your people skills become.

When discussing team leaders in conversations, engineers immediately start listing people they thought lacked the necessary people skills but were nonetheless promoted into positions of influence. True, sometimes technical people are promoted into leadership positions strictly because of their technical abilities, but the question remains—how did it work out? Would *you* want to work with them again? Would you want to be managed by them? Some people slip through the cracks and get those positions because they are *extremely* technically talented, a friend of a vice president, or they were grandfathered in because they were present when the company was founded. The point is their lack of skill with people is a detriment to their overall effectiveness. By changing a handful of key behaviors, they would be more effective and get better results from the people around them. I can only speak for myself, but the people who had the most impact on me were not only technically capable, but were also very good at connecting with and leading others. A good leader does both.

Some engineers are technically gifted but will never be promoted to positions of significant influence because they lack the required people skills to operate on a higher level. Their lack of those skills would be a detriment to their organization.

WHY SHOULD PEOPLE WANT TO FOLLOW YOU?

You may be tempted to look at a leadership position in a one-dimensional way: The leader has the title and authority and all her subordinates are obligated to support her to the best of their abilities. Unfortunately, it often plays out differently in real life. If a person possesses the position, but consistently violates people skills and leadership best practices, the subordinates find it very difficult to put their best work forward because of their personal disdain for the leader. Not many people will go the extra mile for individuals they unequivocally dislike.

In Stephen R. Covey's book *The 7 Habits of Highly Successful People,* he wrote: "You can buy a person's hand, but you can't buy his heart. His heart is where his enthusiasm, his loyalty is. You can buy his back, but you can't buy his brain, that's were his creativity is, his ingenuity his resourcefulness." He points out that not everyone you work with is inspired to operate at their *highest level* simply because they are being paid. Just because you hold the title of leader and your team members receive a paycheck, doesn't mean they are sold on your direction, ideas, or motives and are giving their very best. Sometimes it takes more than money to draw out the best in individuals. Feeling undervalued, underappreciated, or being constantly marginalized all negatively affect individual output and engagement.

As a leader, you may think, "I'm the leader, so people must recognize my position and do what I say." A title can be indicative of your relative position and authority within a company, but if you don't quickly back it up with ability and skill with people, you'll start having people problems in your teams. Running a team based solely on your position is the least effective form of leadership. You can't force people to give you their best because of your position.

In John Maxwell's book *The 5 Levels of Leadership,* he calls leading by rank or title Positional Leadership. Out of the five levels he outlines in his book, Positional Leadership is the very lowest form. He states anyone can lead this way because it takes little skill past being able to issue orders and threats. Even my 12-year-old son could lead that way.

Teams with positional leaders typically have low morale, high turnover, and aren't as effective as they could be because a significant amount of energy is wasted dealing with interpersonal issues. I served four years in the United States Army, an organization that is built completely on the concept of Positional Leadership. It may be the best leadership strategy for an institution that specializes in war, but it's definitely not a good strategy for civilian teams where effort and creativity must be encouraged. Being constantly shut down by people higher on the pecking order simply because of their position gets old really fast.

The more intellectual the members of your teams are, the more time you will spend justifying your decisions. This is normal, so don't get upset when it happens. Your team members *expect* their input to be valued and their concerns to be addressed. When they aren't, they may feel frustration and animosity toward others, especially those in leadership positions. In an engineering organization, great ideas come from everywhere, so it's foolish to ignore what others have to say. As a technical leader, listen to input carefully to avoid relational problems with the team members that could affect team effectiveness. Many engineers only want to make sure their voice was heard and taken into consideration. Once they've aired their grievances and feel they were listened to, they will get on board with whatever the final decision may be.

CONNECT WITH PEOPLE FIRST

You've just been hired on as a software architect for AcmeCatPajamas.com. The company needed someone with your specific skill set, and you are excited to have the opportunity to help the company grow. If everything goes right, this could be a big step toward your ultimate goal of becoming a Chief Technology Officer (CTO) for a medium-to-large tech company. In every way, this new position is a step up for you.

Your first day on the job is filled with standard new-hire activities. You're shown your cube, you get your laptop, and you meet with a few key people in the company who give you the rundown of the current state of affairs. Listening, you begin plotting the new course of the organization you'll be leading. You immediately identify large potential performance gains in parts of the backend services and feel you can create a technical road map to bring the teams up to more standard development processes. You're thinking, "This is going to be good."

Early the next week, you set up a meeting with all the current technical leads in your new organization. Your plan at this meeting is to inform them of the new direction you're taking them and show them why your plan will lay the foundation for future revenue-producing capabilities. After all, it worked at your last company, and you have no reason to believe it won't work here. You are excited to share your vision and can't wait to see how excited everyone else will be when you show them all the future benefits of your design.

On the day of the meeting, all the current technical leads pile into the conference room, anxiously waiting to meet their new leader. You've been there for a while already, making sure the audio and video equipment is working and that your slides are in order. This is your time to shine.

As you start presenting, you notice that some engineers are rolling their eyes during the most impressive points of your technical road map. Immediately, people start voicing their apprehension for your plan, which is a little unsettling to you because they haven't even heard the whole thing yet. In fact, people seem almost openly hostile toward you and your ideas, something you didn't anticipate. "What in the heck is going on?" you think. "Is this just a bad time of the day for meetings?"

After your unproductive meeting ends, you feel deflated. No one seemed excited and some even went so far as to actively reject your direction. Confused, you approach your manager and share your experience. During your conversation, your manager tells you that several of the people at the meeting applied for the very same job you now hold. Replaying the meeting in your mind, you immediately realize the most unsupportive people at your meeting were the same ones who had applied for the position. Could they be harboring ill feelings because they didn't get the job? You convince yourself that is exactly what is happening, but what can you do?

Technical people are notorious for downplaying, or maybe completely ignoring, the role of human nature with regard to team dynamics. Engineers can see things from a binary "this is a better solution, therefore everyone should get behind it" standpoint. Many times, what they don't consider is how grudges, mistrust, and perceived selfish motives affect people's willingness or unwillingness to accept a leader's decisions and directions. Dale Carnegie summed it up perfectly in his classic book *How to Win Friends & Influence People:* "When dealing with people, let us remember we are not dealing with creatures of logic. We are dealing with creatures of emotion, creatures bristling with prejudices and motivated by pride and vanity." If you ignore human nature, you are only making things harder for yourself. People are not computer programs and sometimes behave in very irrational, nondeterministic ways.

In John C. Maxwell's book *The 21 Irrefutable Laws of Leadership,* one of the laws he writes about is called The Law of Buy-In. This law states that people first buy into the leader as a person, *then* they buy into the leader's vision. Many leaders, especially new ones, get things out of order, thus causing themselves much unneeded stress and frustration. Maxwell says in his book: "Once people have bought into someone, they are willing to give his vision a chance. People want to go along with people they get along with." Your first order of business when you are tasked with leading a new team is to *connect with people.*

When first starting to lead individuals in *any* setting, make it your first priority to connect with the individuals on the team. Invite team members over to your house for dinner. Go bowling with them over lunch. Show them that you're interested in learning more about them and that you value them as people. Let them know you're there to help them and the team. Initially, most people don't trust strangers or people they hardly know, so do your best to change that. Do whatever is necessary to no longer be a stranger.

I have a friend where I work who is amazingly smart—one of the smartest people I've met. He was a new hire tasked with leading cross-functional teams within the company. Right off the bat, he started experiencing relational problems with the engineers he was supposed to be leading. The problems were significant enough that he was referred to me, and we started meeting every week to go through much of the same material I'm covering in this book. As we started discussing some best practices, he began having what are typically referred to as "aha moments." He acknowledged he was trying to lead people before he had connected with them, which caused strife between him and the people he was supposed to be helping. The people hadn't accepted him as a leader yet. What did he do? He simply put the brakes on, started personally connecting more with them, and the situation changed almost immediately. The exact same approach will work for you, too. If you were to talk to my friend, he would tell you the exact same thing I'm telling you: Focus on connecting with people first, because that's the platform you'll use to successfully lead them later. Learn from my friend's experience.

If you come into a team "guns a blazin'," prepare to encounter difficulties. This is especially true when you don't know the people you are attempting to lead. If you try to lead without first communicating to people that you have their best interests at heart, they will be less apt to trust you and the direction you are trying to take them. Hear my words: *Failing to connect with people you're trying to lead will only make your job that much more difficult.* You don't have to be best friends, but spend the necessary time building trust and getting to know the people on your team before plotting a new course for them. This is a basic leadership skill you'll find in most any leadership book written in the past ten to twenty years. Don't make the same mistake so many other leaders do. Connect first and everything else will have a higher probability of working.

LISTEN FIRST, THEN DECIDE

Good technical leaders listen. They listen a lot. The engineers on your team want to be heard and know that their input was considered during the decision-making process. They don't necessarily have to get their way; they simply want to know that their input was considered. Failing to listen, or making decisions behind closed doors with little or no input from your team members, is a surefire way to stir up dissensions and frustration. As highly paid technical workers, engineers *expect* their opinions and input to matter. When their leaders marginalize them, it makes them angry.

From a practical standpoint, team members understand who has the ultimate decision-making authority, so you're not giving away your authority by listening to them. Listening to their input doesn't make you less of a leader; it makes you more effective because you don't have to slog through waist-deep people problems while trying to design solutions to very complicated problems. Technical leaders don't have the time or extra energy available to fight constant interpersonal fires—they have too much work to do. Time spent ignoring basic leadership principles, and dealing with the fallout from it, is time not spent delivering product features.

Simply telling people what to do doesn't involve them in the solution, which means they are less invested. Stephen R. Covey says it this way: "Without involvement, there is no commitment. Mark it down, asterisk it, circle it, underline it. No involvement, no commitment." Without involvement in the decision-making process, some engineers will never take true ownership of the solution. You want your team to not only share in the rewards that come with delivering at a high level, but also know their reputation as a team is on the line if things don't work out. You want them personally invested in the results. The best way to do this is to include your team when designing solutions.

Engineers take a fair amount of math courses in college. It's common for professors to assign odd-numbered homework problems so students can look in the back of the book and check their answers. This approach is helpful because it's easy to mess up a minus sign or make a simple mistake on one of the dozens (or hundreds) of calculations involved in solving a single problem. While solving problems, students can check their answers in the back and then run through the process again until they find the correct solution. How helpful would it be to go directly to the back of the book for the answer without first going through the process of solving the problem? Sure, the correct answer is there, but the student would have no idea how to solve similar problems on their own when no book is available. The same can be said about designing solutions together with your team.

If you're a team leader, you probably possess experience and an innate ability that others don't. Don't hoard that ability. Instead, teach others what you know and show them how to solve the difficult problems you're facing. Showing up to a team meeting to present a solution you designed in isolation is analogous to finding the answer in the back of the book. You may have arrived at the correct answer, but your team didn't learn the process you used to reach the correct solution. When faced with similar problems in the future, they won't know what to do. As a leader, use every opportunity to train those around you. The more they know, the better they can make decentralized decisions. It's like cloning yourself; whenever you take the time to teach your team members, you deposit some of your decision-making abilities in them. As a result, their decisions get better, and your need to inject yourself into the team's daily workflow should become less and less. This frees you up to focus on the next set of solutions. When the tide rises, all the boats go up!

Something that might not be obvious to every technical leader reading this book is that the people on your team may have better ideas than you. Or, as I like to say, "No one has the market cornered on good ideas." One of the biggest benefits of listening to others' input before making decisions is that the overall quality of the solution may be better because of their input. You work with smart people. Why wouldn't you want their input? It's quite possible the 23-year-old new hire has an idea that could revolutionize your product.

'I'M NOT TONY STARK'

There is a scene in the 2008 movie *Iron Man* where Obadiah Stane (the villain played by Jeff Bridges) corners one of his scientists and asks about the status of the replica Iron Man suit Obadiah is trying to build. The scientist explains that the technology to power the suit doesn't exist yet and Obadiah responds by yelling "Tony Stark was able to build this in a cave! With a box of scraps!" The scientist, a little shaken by the exchange, calmly replies, "Well I'm sorry, I'm not Tony Stark."

As a technical lead, you may sometimes forget that not everyone has the same technical ability and skills you do. In fact, you may have been promoted into your current position *because* you possess uncommon or advanced engineering ability. If you're not careful, you might expect too much out of the people working with you. This isn't to say you shouldn't continually stretch others by helping them push the limits of their capabilities; but if you're not careful, you may expect more out of them than they are able to give at this point in their career.

People have varying degrees of ability and talent. In a team environment, some people are naturally going to be better and smarter than others. You run into problems when you have unrealistic expectations and believe that everyone should be as good as you are, completely disregarding your innate ability, past experiences, and passion for the work. You should identify where everyone is at on your team, then do your best to mentor them without making them feel somehow inferior because they are not as good as you.

You never want to rub people's noses in your superior ability. In the end, doing so will cause resentment. Humility is key. Everyone is probably already aware of your abilities based on the work you do. Gifted technical people naturally percolate up through the ranks and establish a reputation for having advanced abilities.

Here's some advice about how to conduct yourself in a team environment: Don't seek to impress others, just be impressive. Let your conduct and results speak for themselves. People already know if you're the superstar of your team.

SUMMARY

> Successfully leading other people is largely dependent upon your character and skill with people.

> Positional Leadership (leading by rank or title) is the lowest form of leadership.

> People first buy into the leader as a person, and then they buy into the leader's vision. Spend time connecting with people before trying to lead them.

> Without involvement, there is no commitment. Good technical leaders include their teams in the decision-making process.

> Teach others how to solve problems instead of designing solutions in isolation. You want to create new future leaders, not more followers.

> Stretch your people, but don't have unrealistic

expectations. Not everyone will be as technically gifted as you, and that's OK. Stretch, but don't break them.

CHAPTER 7

How to Avoid and Resolve Conflict

The longer I teach this material, the more convinced I have become that people are suffering in their relationships at work not because they need some newfangled approach to solving the problems they face, but because they are not doing many of the basics correctly. It's easy to substitute knowing for doing, and as a result, we *think* we are doing things right; but in reality, we either stopped practicing the good behaviors or never did them long enough for them to be of any benefit to us. Because of this, we could continually look for new approaches to our problems, since we think we've already tried everything else and it doesn't work. It's possible that we've done *some* of the good behaviors *some* of the time, but we haven't made them habits; and because of this, we aren't experiencing the benefits of them.

In one episode of the MTV show *Beavis and Butthead,* they were lifting weights for what seemed like only a few minutes before going back into the locker room. They took off their shirts, looked in the mirror, and marveled at how much bigger they were. The obvious joke was

Beavis and Butthead thought they had put on a bunch of muscle mass after lifting weights one time, which we know isn't the way it works. If we want to get good at anything, we need to do the right things often enough and long enough that they will benefit us.

Author Robert Bolton summed it up perfectly: "To be human is to experience conflict." If you're around other people, you'll have nearly limitless opportunities to experience conflict. The Merriam-Webster Dictionary defines conflict as:

> *conflict:* mental struggle resulting from incompatible or opposing needs, drives, wishes, or external or internal demands

Simply put, when we have problems with people, we experience conflict. Unfortunately, it is impossible to completely avoid all conflict. Regardless of whether we think we are doing everything right on our end, we will run into problems because we can't control what other people say and do. Therefore, we have three options available to us when experiencing conflict:

1. Run away from it.
2. Deal with it poorly.
3. Deal with it wisely.

Conflict comes in many forms, such as disagreements, arguments, and personality conflicts, to name a few. Not all conflict is bad. For instance, many disagreements are perfectly healthy and should be a part of our daily interactions, especially in the workplace. Civil disagreements are the foundry for great ideas and help bring to light deficiencies in current practices. A workplace without welcomed disagreements is probably not a very fun place to work because it means people don't feel empowered to disagree, usually because of fear. Disagreements, even heated ones, are valuable as long as they do not stay unresolved. Unresolved conflict poisons any environment, whether at home, at work, or as a volunteer.

In this chapter, we'll cover the foundational principles that should be applied to situations where we *start* to experience conflict with others. As soon as a problem begins to appear, it needs to be addressed. Typically, the sooner you address interpersonal problems, the easier they are to deal with. Given enough time, problems that could have been handled in a few minutes grow into figurative monsters that can end up destroying teams and putting wedges between people. Handle the problem when it's small, so it doesn't grow so big you need reinforcements to handle it.

WE HAVE A 'BANK ACCOUNT' WITH OTHER PEOPLE

In Stephen Covey's *The 7 Habits of Highly Effective People,* he presents an abstract concept about our standing with other people and compares it to a bank account. Because most people are familiar with bank accounts, this analogy gives a little more insight into your personal interactions with the people around you and shows where you might be off.

When you open a bank account with a financial institution, you can start making deposits into or withdrawals from it. If you put money in, you can get the money out at a later date. If you try to withdraw too much, at best you can't get what you want, and at worst, you get charged an overdraft fee. Just as a bank account works from a financial standpoint, our bank accounts with people work in a similar way.

With every interaction, you either make a deposit into or a withdrawal from the individual you're interacting with. Every time you ask someone for something, you make a withdrawal—sometimes small, sometimes large. Every time you marginalize or criticize someone, you make a withdrawal. Eventually, if you haven't made enough deposits into a person's account, your account becomes overdrawn (insufficient funds), and that's when you start experiencing problems.

When certain people approach you, do you ever think to yourself,

"Oh great, what did I do wrong now?" Whenever you do something right, they are nowhere to be found. But when you mess up, they seem to materialize out of thin air to inform you of your mistake. The problem with the way this person is behaving is that they only make withdrawals from your account without putting in any deposits. The relationship is strained due to insufficient funds in one or both of your accounts. Neither of you is getting the best out of each other when things reach this point.

Do you have strained relationships at work? Does it seem like the people around you stop contributing to discussions when you're present? Do co-workers try to actively avoid you? If so, your bank account with these individuals might be running low. How do you fix it? You start by intentionally making deposits to build up your reserves with the people, so when you need to make a withdrawal, your account can handle it. If you put it off until you need the interpersonal capital, it's too late. For example, make people feel important by praising *specific* things they've done recently. Stop by their workspace to ask how they are doing in a casual conversation. The deposit doesn't have to be huge. People are so starved for positive human affirmation that nearly anything is a giant leap in the right direction.

When I worked for a large technology company as a software engineer, I had to consciously make deposits into an individual's account to patch up a rough first impression he had of me. We got off to a bad start, and I knew that without intervention, it was going to stay bad and potentially get worse.

Alex was a good employee, a bit rough around the edges, but a good guy in most respects. He was a hard worker and genuinely wanted to do the right thing for the company. When I was first introduced to him, I was overly aggressive when discussing the direction I thought the team should go. Looking back, I was too energetic in my approach and said things I shouldn't have. I could tell immediately that he didn't particularly like what I had to say because his demeanor changed. From then on, he never talked much when I was around, and the way he carried himself was much more reserved. I realized I'd hurt him.

I had a choice to make. I could forget about it and hope my relationship with Alex got better on its own, or I could proactively try to patch things up using the limited skills I had at the time. I knew from experience that most people aren't very good about forgiving and moving on, so it was probably going to fall on me to fix the problem (which is probably the right thing, since it was my mouth that caused the issue in the first place). I immediately got to work thinking about how I could build up my bank account with him.

Looking back, patching up the relationship was much easier than I thought it would be. I stopped by his cube every other day or so and told him how good of a job he was doing (if warranted), or I'd ask him questions about his personal life to get to know him a little better. I made an effort to deposit into his account, and it worked! Because of those simple deposits, he started smiling every time he saw me, and he'd even stop by my cube occasionally just to strike up a conversation. After a month or so, he may have even considered me a friend.

A lot of the stressful relationships at work can be improved with a simple game plan for how to go about making the correct deposits into the other person's account. I recognize that every relationship won't be as easy to fix as the example I just gave, but I've never seen a relationship hurt by trying to build someone up. Actively manage your accounts with others and continually make the necessary deposits so that when you need to make a withdrawal, there will be plenty of "money" in the account.

YOU REAP WHAT YOU SOW

The principle of sowing and reaping has been known by people for thousands of years. A very simple explanation of it goes something like this: Whatever you "sow" (give, do, say, etc.) is exactly what you will "reap" (have returned to you). Sometimes people refer to it as karma or "what goes around, comes around."

Picture this scenario. A farmer goes to the local supply store and buys corn seeds. He comes home and, after confidently preparing the soil in his garden, purposely plants his corn seeds in nice, straight rows perfectly distanced apart, so each one of his plants will have just the right amount of space to flourish. After planting, he begins to water his seeds. Weeks go by, and the plants start to break through the soil and grow. Quickly, they are a few feet high. The farmer, having left for a couple of weeks on a much-needed vacation (do farmers take vacations?), walks out to his field, takes a look at his crop, and says, "Where are all my tomatoes?"

What would you tell the farmer? You'd probably tell him, "If you wanted tomatoes, you shouldn't have planted corn seeds." This story may seem a little ridiculous, but people operate the same way in their daily lives. They plant one kind of seed and expect to reap a different kind of crop.

All day long, you plant different kinds of seeds in your gardens, not realizing that just as assuredly as planting corn seeds in a physical garden will produce corn plants, the seeds we plant with other people will also produce after the types of seeds planted. This law is massive in its application because it affects so many different areas. Think of all the interactions you have with the people you work with. Each of these interactions is an opportunity to sow a seed with them.

If you had a garden in your backyard, it would take less than one minute for anyone to tell you exactly what kinds of seeds you planted based on what's growing. You could argue with the person, tell them there's no way you planted a certain kind of vegetable, but in the end, the garden speaks for itself. Corn seeds have not produced, do not produce, nor will they ever produce tomato plants. What's growing in your garden is exactly what you planted, whether you choose to acknowledge it or not.

If your work life is full of strained relationships, strife, and confrontational interactions with co-workers, others can tell exactly what kinds of seeds you planted. They wouldn't have to be there when you put the seed in the ground. They can see the results for themselves.

If you want to be more skillful at dealing with people, you cannot continue to plant the same bad seeds year after year and expect to get different results. It doesn't work that way. The only way to get better results is to sow the right seeds to get the things you want to receive in return—patience, understanding, support, and help.

THINK ABOUT WHAT YOU SAY BEFORE YOU SAY IT

Most computer applications have keyboard shortcuts to simplify commonly used commands. In many programs, CTRL+Z (or the program-specific equivalent) is the shortcut for the undo command and is typically one of the favorite shortcuts of most users. If you make a mistake, you press CTRL+Z and correct it. If you make a *bunch* of mistakes, you press CTRL+Z a *bunch* of times. Because of this key combination, you don't have to worry much because you can always undo the mistake you made and do it again the right way.

Unfortunately, life doesn't have a CTRL+Z keyboard shortcut. Because of the lack of an undo command, sometimes all you get is one time to do or say the right thing. Saying the wrong thing at the wrong time can create problems for you well past the original verbal transgression.

The undisciplined use of words is one of the worst things you can do to yourself from a career perspective. Your mouth possesses so much destructive capability that it would be complete foolishness to not put strict controls on its use. Not actively managing your words is like walking around with a loaded handgun everywhere you go, pointing and waving it at people. You would never do that. Why? Because you respect the weapon and the damage it can cause. Your words should be treated with the same respect because they possess just as much killing power.

Just like bullets fired from a gun, once you choose your words and say them, there is no taking them back. You can apologize, but the damage is still done. Some words are so divisive that the wounds they cause may never fully heal. For the other engineers around you, the undisciplined use of your mouth can be nearly unbearable and cause long-term, deep-rooted resentment toward you. Be careful! Once your word-bullets are fired, there's no getting them back. As engineers, let us apply the same careful thinking we use to respond to technical problems to our personal interactions with others.

DON'T CRITICIZE OR COMPLAIN

Most people are familiar with Nike's slogan, "Just do it!" Here's a good slogan when it comes to criticism, "Criticism—don't do it!" So, what does it mean to criticize? A quick Google search defines criticize this way:

> *criticize: indicate the faults of (someone or something) in a disapproving way*

Synonyms of criticize include condemn, attack, lambaste, rail against, pour scorn on, disparage, denigrate, give bad press to, and run down. These are all bad actions, and operating this way has negative implications on your interactions with others.

Let there be no mistake about this: *Criticism's sole purpose is to run down or wound another person.* It's mean-spirited and typically is used as an outlet for anger and frustration. It damages relationships and creates problems in organizations. As engineering professionals, we don't want to criticize people to their faces or behind their backs.

As leaders and managers, we sometimes need to correct people we are supervising. Correction is normal, is one of the primary responsibilities of leaders, and can be done in such a way that our intent is conveyed and the recipient of the correction saves face. Criticism, as a form of correction, is the opposite. Its goal is to inflict enough damage to another person that he or she will obey out of fear (wanting to avoid further criticism). It's used liberally in top-down organizations like the military and can be effective at getting a quick fix to a problem. After all, who likes to be run down in front of other people? There are much more effective forms of correction available to us, though, such as inspiration, encouragement, and mentorship, to name a few. These forms have less negative, long-term repercussions than criticism.

If you choose to criticize, you lose the goodwill of the person you're criticizing. Instead of having an ally, you have a potential enemy. Criticize someone enough and you're likely to find yourself in a situation where a person not only wants to see you fail but will do everything in their power to see it come to pass. It creates an adversarial environment in the workplace and is counterproductive. Think about the Opportunity Tree mentioned at the beginning of the book. Continually criticizing a person damages that branch of your tree. Do you think your co-worker will recommend you for a future job opportunity if all you've done is criticize them for the last two years? No way! People don't realize how many opportunities pass them by because of things like this.

I have worked with many software engineers over the past sixteen years who have made it their personal duty to criticize the work of everyone else around them. Typically, they are smart and gifted at what they do and use that as their license to tear down everyone else. I suspect this phenomenon is not specific to developing software, either. As a result, the very people whom everyone else should be seeking out for help and support are approached with reluctance because no one wants to deal with their abrasive personality. Sound familiar? They have created small barriers in the organization, and as a result, the team isn't as effective as it could be.

Criticism is counterproductive and wastes a lot of time and emotional energy because it makes people defensive. You may have experienced this scenario firsthand during something like a weekly staff meeting. As people explain what they've been working on, someone decides to criticize an individual. At this point, the person being criticized enters survival mode and is more concerned with saving face than having a productive meeting. An entire meeting can be wasted on a couple of people going back-and-forth trying to justify the decisions they made.

Many people take criticisms personally regardless of your intentions. They treat it like you're picking a fight with them. Even if you play the constructive-criticism card and say you're trying to help them by giving them negative feedback, people don't like it. As a rule, people never like to be told they are wrong and never like to be criticized for anything they do. That doesn't mean you can't correct someone; it means you must be careful how you do it. If you choose to ignore human nature, you're setting the odds against you. Use your understanding of human nature to your advantage. Get the results you want and build stronger teams while you're at it. You can be skillful at dealing with people *and* have the most productive team in your organization.

In addition to damaging relationships, criticism is also the single biggest killer of the creative process. If you allow any amount of criticism in team settings, some engineers will stop participating or limit their participation out of fear of being criticized, which has a direct impact on the quality of your decisions and solutions. As Dave Hendricksen, the author of *12 Essential Skills for Software Architects,* put it: "Normally, the first few ideas that people throw out are 'safe' ideas. They are testing the waters to see if sharks are present. If it proves to be safe, they are willing to begin bringing out their best and brightest ideas." If you are a shark, or allow sharks on your team, you won't fully harness the creative abilities of everyone. *Do not allow criticism.* If you want the best out of people, create a safe environment that is conducive to the free exchange of opposing viewpoints.

If you feel like criticizing someone else, stop and ask yourself what your motive is. Are you trying to make yourself look better, or are you trying to help the other person? No one is perfect. You could criticize everyone for plenty of things, but why? What's the end game? Instead, look for healthy ways to encourage and correct the individual. Tools for how to properly correct people are discussed in a later chapter titled "How to Correct People."

When talking about criticism, people often like to point to individuals whose style of leadership runs contrary to what we are talking about but were successful in spite of it. The prior CEO of Apple, Steve Jobs, falls into this category. First, let me say that there is, and will only ever be, one Steve Jobs. The guy was a tech visionary and, to my understanding, did things his own way from the beginning. Modeling your leadership style after someone like him is like modeling your retirement after a lottery winner—if you think your retirement will be funded by lottery winnings, it's not going to work out for you.

What will work out for you, from both a leadership and retirement perspective? Fundamentals. That's right, the good old fundamentals of dealing with people and the fundamentals of investing for retirement. Don't bet your retirement on winning the lottery, and don't bet your ability to influence people on a one-in-a-million personality. Stick with what works for the other 99.9 percent of people. Be a tech visionary *and* be the most skillful people person at your company.

If you want people to dislike you, criticize them, especially in front of others. Or, if you'd rather not openly promote strife and contentions in the workplace, make the decision to avoid criticizing others. You get better results when you don't actively create friction between yourself and those around you. The goal for most people is to get better results. Stopping criticism in its tracks, in every area of your life, will move you closer to that objective.

Along with criticism, complaining is another one of those unsavory activities engineers may be tempted to engage in.

> ***complain:*** *express dissatisfaction or annoyance about a state of affairs or an event*

Synonyms of complain include grumble and whine. You can see why this is an undesirable way to conduct yourself. Who wants to be known for being a whiner?

From a practical standpoint, people don't like being around complainers. These people are constantly focused on the negative in any situation and make sure everyone else knows about it, too. They *find* something to complain about just to strike up a conversation. They suck the life out of everyone around them and sometimes are actively avoided for that reason.

Complaining adds absolutely no value to any interaction, so it should be avoided altogether. The negative is always going to be around. That's unavoidable. What you can control is how you respond to it and what you choose to focus on.

Instead of complaining, use your words to make deposits into the bank accounts of the people around you. The people most admired are not complainers, but problem solvers. If a situation isn't right, they find a way to fix it. If they can't fix it, they figure out what they *can* do and focus on that instead. That's why people like them and they have more influence on those around them. Endeavor to be like that yourself.

Complaining is a drag on everyone involved. If your team is in the middle of a rough patch, everyone already knows. People aren't interested in being beat over the head with complaints. What they are interested in is how their current situation is going to change and get back on track. Developing a plan, executing on the plan, and course-correcting along the way accomplishes change, not complaining. People admire others who stay positive in the midst of any situation.

FORGIVE PEOPLE WHEN THEY DO STUPID THINGS

If we work around people long enough, they *will* occasionally say and do things that wound us on a personal level. Some engineers may even be downright mean-spirited and vindictive toward us—they intentionally are trying to inflict damage on us. Maybe we know why, maybe we don't. The good news is that regardless of their motives, we have complete control over how we respond to the attack on our character, abilities, or performance.

Forgiveness is a powerful character trait that all engineers should possess. Forgiveness will keep you from getting bogged down in a lot of unnecessary relational baggage. When you choose not to forgive someone, it's like throwing a rock into your backpack. You might be able to handle a few rocks, but after a while, the backpack becomes completely unmanageable. If you refuse to put rocks in your backpack, everything you do gets a lot easier since you aren't hauling around a bunch of "state" (baggage from previous interactions). Just like a properly designed web service, you should also strive to be stateless (not holding on to grudges) with the people around you.

A lot of people don't want to forgive because they view it as letting someone off the hook. They view it as saying to the other person, "What you did to me is OK, I forgive you." That's not what forgiveness is. When you forgive someone, you are not condoning the behavior, but are severing the cord between the offense and you. You no longer give it any power over you. You are releasing that person from any control or influence over you and are effectively washing your hands of the situation. Think of it as releasing a balloon into the air and walking away. It's gone, and it's not coming back. Forgiveness is a healthy way to deal with offense without it negatively affecting your career.

Forgiving someone doesn't mean you have to be friends. You may think that if you forgive someone, the relationship moves forward as if the offense never took place. This isn't true. Forgiving someone doesn't mean you pretend the bad thing never happened. Not at all. For example, if a certain manager is overly critical and aggressive every time you talk, you may want to limit your exposure to that manager, if possible. Common sense still applies while you're trying to become more skillful with people.

You may not want to forgive because you want revenge and want the other person to feel as bad as you do. That strategy usually doesn't work. Revenge only makes matters worse and doesn't fix the original problem. Sure, it might make you feel better for a moment, but the anger typically remains and continues to build up again once your revenge fix has worn off.

Bottled-up anger slowly eats you from the inside out. All that stress and negative emotion comes out in some form. It either comes out as forgiveness, which is healthy, or it manifests itself as health problems or destructive behavior. Don't keep things bottled up inside thinking that if you forgive the other person, they somehow win. That person probably doesn't spend one second thinking about what was said or done to you. You're the only one affected. Any time you choose not to forgive someone, you're the loser and not the person who did you wrong.

Forgiveness isn't conditional. It doesn't depend on an apology first. If you wait for someone to apologize, you might be waiting for a very long time. In fact, some people will never apologize—they will literally die first. What then? Do you want to carry around the ill feelings toward the person for the rest of your life? That's why proactively forgiving people is so powerful! You don't need another person's apology to forgive; all you need to do is make the decision to forgive. You have the power to diffuse a situation without help from anyone else. It's impossible to keep people down who quickly forgive others on a continual basis. They refuse to put the rocks in their backpacks that would otherwise slow them down.

I'm not trying to trivialize or make light of the bad things that happen to people. All I'm trying to say is what are your options? If someone did or said something stupid, you can't build a time machine and go back in time to prevent it from happening. All we have is now. You can either deal with the problem and forgive, or keep dragging it around and have it affect your future.

ADMIT YOUR MISTAKES AND APOLOGIZE, IF NECESSARY

Everybody is wrong on occasion. What separates the mature engineer from the immature engineer is how you handle the situation when it happens. Do you use the situation to gain influence with the people around you, or do you lose some of their respect? Believe it or not, you can make mistakes and come out looking better for it by applying the following principles. You may have to swallow your pride, but those who do so are the types of people others like to associate with.

If you know you're wrong, admit it. Odds are others know you're wrong, too. People respect you more when they see you mess up and admit it. It shows that you know you're not perfect and you're willing to improve. The longer you go without admitting your mistake, the more damage you do to yourself in the eyes of the people around you. Nobody likes to be around someone who is so prideful or self-righteous that they won't admit when they're wrong. Mature people humble themselves and confess the fact that they miss the mark sometimes.

If you're wrong all the time, you may have a different kind of problem altogether. Just like people don't like it if you never admit your mistakes, they also don't like it if you're wrong all the time. They lose confidence in your judgment. If you're habitually wrong, maybe you're in the wrong position in your organization. Maybe you need more training or experience under your belt in your current position. People will give you some leeway if you're coming up to speed in an area, but they eventually expect you to positively contribute without having to second-guess everything you say and do. Maybe you simply need to talk less or think more about what to say before you say it.

It's OK if you're not perfect. Some people seem to think that it's an unforgivable sin to be wrong. It isn't. It's called being human. Our goal should be to continually drive those mistakes out of our lives, but there will always be some situations in which we say or do the wrong thing—it's just a part of life. Don't put such a heavy burden on yourself that you think you have to be correct 100 percent of the time. You don't, so don't become your own worst critic. Nobody is keeping a list of the number of times you've made mistakes—only you are.

When you make a mistake, learn from it, and find out how to prevent it from happening in the future. Learning from your mistakes gives you something positive and encouraging to take away from the experience and takes some of the sting out of the mistake itself. If you are constantly trying to grow yourself and do new things, making mistakes is part of the game. If you never make any mistakes, you may be operating in an area where you're comfortable, and there probably isn't much room left in that area for personal growth. Get out into some new areas! Don't let mistakes discourage you from growing.

The second principle to apply when you make a mistake is to follow up your confession with an apology, if necessary. If you need to apologize, do it. Don't make excuses. Don't try to blame it on someone else. If you've done something wrong to someone, sincerely apologize and move on. Own your mistake and do whatever is in your power to make it right. Don't let things linger for months or years because that causes too many unneeded problems in the meantime.

The longer you go without apologizing, the worse things can get. If you've slighted others in some way, apologize as soon as possible to prevent things like gossip from occurring. You don't want people to go around and say potentially damaging things about you to others simply because you didn't apologize when you should have. If you acknowledge your error and sincerely apologize, most people will genuinely accept your apology and move on.

ASK QUESTIONS TO AVOID UNNECESSARY CONFLICT

You might be surprised how effective a couple of well-thought-out questions can be at guiding people to their own mistakes while avoiding counterproductive person-to-person conflict. In many cases, asking questions like "What are your plans if situation X pops up?" are much better than the alternative "Your solution doesn't address all of the problems. It won't work." This is because the second statement creates a defensive atmosphere and promotes problems between people. Even if you know something is wrong or there is a better way to do a particular thing, it still pays to ask questions. It's worth the time and effort to create a healthy atmosphere for helping others to see their own mistakes without creating conflict.

If you constantly tell people they're wrong, you may be wasting a lot of potential influence with people. If you're very capable at what you do, think how effective you could be with that knowledge and the ability to guide people to a solution while avoiding interpersonal strife. You'd become a figurative superhero that others go to for guidance, not only because you could help them see a better way of doing things, but because you would do it in a way that lets them keep their dignity. People who already respect your technical ability will also respect the way you help others in your organization accomplish goals without running people down. You expand your influence with others and open new doors of opportunity for advancement.

By asking questions, you include others in finding a solution to a problem, which in turn gives them a piece of ownership of the final deliverable. As a technical leader, you can get more involvement and commitment out of your team by simply having them help you design the solutions to the complex issues your team faces. This makes a big difference when it comes to facilitating more teamwork and cooperation amongst individuals.

If you constantly tell others what to do, it's not their solution they are implementing—it's *your* solution. If the solution fails, *your* solution failed, and the majority of the fault is yours. If the solution developed by the team fails, the team as a whole fails. Do you see the difference? In the first instance, they never had true ownership of any piece of it. If you involve your people in the decision-making process, you are more likely to get that true buy-in that leaders say they want. Why? Because the people doing the work now have a real sense of ownership of their piece—they helped design it.

Asking good questions almost completely liberates you from having to be the bad guy. Instead of being the person who decides something isn't possible, you can lead the team to that conclusion by asking the right questions so they can see why a decision needs to be made a certain way. You might think, "But isn't that just a big waste of time?" It depends on how much you value the long-term goodwill of the people around you. For good leaders, it's not just about getting the most efficient solution as quickly as possible, it's about long-term influence and mentorship.

Using questions to lead people where you want them to go is a great way to foster an atmosphere of inclusion in your organization. Questions put others in the driver's seat, which gives them an opportunity to voice their opinions and say what they would do if they were making the final decision. Instead of just following orders, you're making them think about what they're doing. This will grow technical leaders, and is an easy way to make your team members feel valued. It's another small way you can gain influence with others and strengthen your relationships with them.

REFUSE TO BE OFFENDED

You get to choose how you respond to circumstances at work, and no one can take that away from you. Regardless of what someone says or does, you decide how to respond to it. Figure 3 is a visual representation of that decision.

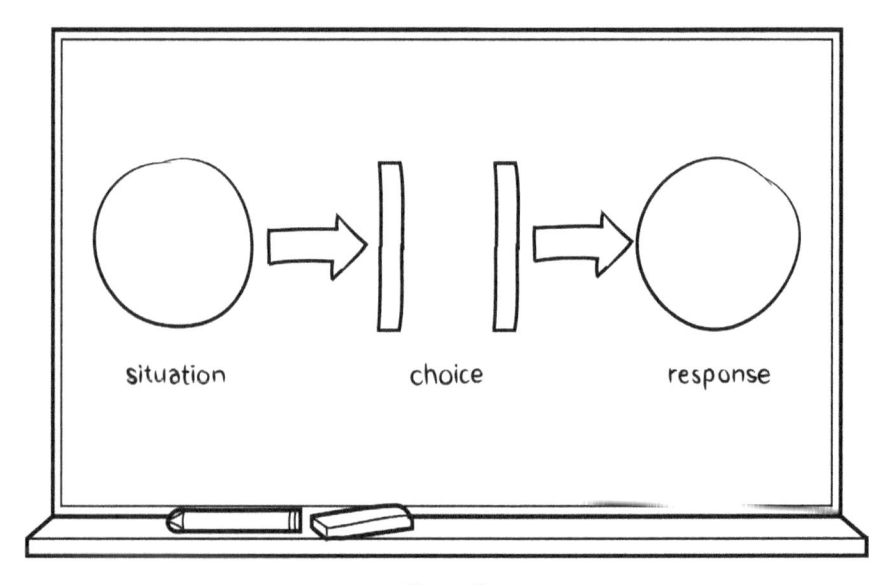

Figure 3

If you make a poor, hasty decision because of what another person says or does, you have no one else to blame but yourself. No one can make you take offense to something—you choose to be offended. Part of growing as an engineer is understanding that your reactions to circumstances are completely within your control. If you understand this truth, you'll make more good decisions, and those good decisions will affect you in a more positive way.

Wherever there are people, there are opportunities to be offended. It's not realistic for you to completely avoid other people, so it stands to reason that the better you are at dealing with offense, the more successful you're going to be as an engineer. While not condoning offensive behavior, you prevent it from affecting your career in a negative way. Why give someone else that much control over you?

Don't let offensive people or situations dictate how far you go in your career. The higher you go within your organization, the bigger of a target you become. If you leave companies and walk away from teams and projects every time someone says or does something offensive, you're choosing to exempt yourself from reaching the highest levels of success in your career. You may as well forget about significantly influencing any sizable group of people, because eventually, some of them are going to do things that could offend you, *if* you allowed it. Don't allow it.

DON'T ARGUE

Arguing should not be confused with the civil exchange of opposing viewpoints, which is a very common part of developing solutions to problems. Instead, arguing is when you see red, your emotions take over, and you lose control of your logic and reasoning. Google defines argument as:

> ***argument:*** *an exchange of diverging or opposite views, typically a heated or angry one*

This type of interaction is usually fueled by anger and results in hurt feelings and sometimes irreparable damage to relationships. In my adult life, I've had a few of these interactions with people. I can say, without a doubt, that I have regretted every single one of them, so much so that if I ever build a time machine, I plan to go back in time and prevent myself from engaging in them. I've had arguments with my wife during the two decades we've been married and always end up apologizing. It's embarrassing and not something I have ever been proud of. What have I learned? Don't argue.

Arguments create barriers and cannot be won. So much collateral damage can be caused in a heated argument that even if you present a stronger logical case for your point of view, the amount of long-term goodwill you lose from the other person makes your victory hollow and worthless. You may have made your point, but you are now at odds with your co-worker. Is it worth it?

Alcoholics Anonymous teaches a warning system called HALT. Each letter in HALT stands for a physical or emotional condition:

> **H**ungry
> **A**ngry
> **L**onely
> **T**ired

Whenever you are experiencing one of these feelings, you're the most vulnerable to making poor decisions. Recovering addicts are more likely to relapse during these times. Avoid making any important decisions or engaging in a heated discussion when you are hungry, angry, lonely, or tired. Instead, cool down, get something to eat, and perhaps sleep on it before you decide what to do.

When you're angry, you may lose that filter that keeps you from saying things you know you'll regret later. Without this filter in place, you're at the mercy of your emotions, and that's a bad place to be. Your first response to anger is often wanting to retaliate and hurt another person. You may say mean, hurtful, and destructive things. Once spoken, those words cannot be taken back. If you don't stop yourself, you may say things that will adversely affect your relationships and ultimately your career.

In the book *Crucial Conversations,* the authors Patterson, Grenny, McMillan, and Switzler outline additional consequences of engaging in unsafe (threatening) interactions. The first consequence involves the physical effects of the interaction on your body. When your emotions crank up, your body literally prepares to enter fight-or-flight mode. In preparation, key brain functions start shutting down to combat the perceived threat. The authors say when you genuinely feel threatened, you develop tunnel vision and "have a hard time seeing beyond the point you're trying to make." When you feel an argument coming on, you lose perspective and may not think clearly, which is precisely the *wrong* time to engage in this type of interaction.

When people begin to feel unsafe, angry, or worked up, they typically choose one of two responses to the situation: silence or violence. As a professional looking for solutions to difficult problems, how can you get the best out of your team if people stop participating or become aggressive toward each other?

As this chapter comes to a close, you need to understand one thing: Your goal shouldn't be to become a spineless pushover who avoids all confrontations because they make you feel uncomfortable. Instead, be aware of how certain behaviors affect those around you and choose your responses to circumstances based on that knowledge. Instead of parroting bad behavior exhibited by individuals who may be completely ignorant of the principles in this book, be deliberate with your interactions with others. Some behaviors have known bad side effects. To avoid the negative side effects of those behaviors, train yourself not to engage in them. Interact with others in a way that will have a direct, positive effect on team productivity and effectiveness so that you bring all your organization's effectiveness to the table. Just like when trying to come up with sound engineering solutions, use the same rigor and attention to detail when designing solutions to your interpersonal problems because both technical and non-technical skills contribute to the success of the *overall* solution.

SUMMARY

> A certain amount of conflict is unavoidable because we can't directly control others. We have three choices when dealing with conflict:
>
>   1. Run away from it.
>   2. Deal with it poorly.
>   3. Deal with it wisely.

> The bank account analogy gives you insight into the state of your relationships. Are you always making withdrawals from those around you? Do you have a plan for making deposits?

> The adage is true: You reap what you sow. What kinds of seeds are you sowing with your co-workers?

> There is no CTRL+Z (undo) in life. Think about what you say *before* you say it. Some words and actions can cause long-term, deep-rooted resentments.

> Criticisms can be viewed as personal attacks. Avoid

making them. Criticism also shuts down creativity.

- Complaining sucks the life out of everyone around you.

- Engineers do dumb things sometimes. When this happens, be the first to forgive so that you're not carrying around any relational baggage.

- If you're wrong, admit it. You can gain trust and respect by admitting your mistakes.

- Ask the right questions to lead people to their mistakes.

- When other engineers say and do offensive things, refuse to receive the offense. You have a choice to let the offensive behavior rent space in your brain or not.

- Arguments can't be won. Be aware of your physical and emotional state before engaging in tense and heated discussions. HALT! Avoid arguments, especially during times when you're hungry, angry, lonely, or tired.

CHAPTER 8

Appreciate People and Make Them Feel Important

People are chronically underappreciated. Because of this, the rare individuals who take it upon themselves to liberally appreciate people in their lives have a huge advantage. Since many people tend to be self-focused, they miss countless opportunities to positively contribute to the quality of life of the people around them. Being more appreciative of people can significantly change your relationships for the better, especially if you don't do much of it now.

If you take people for granted long enough, you will eventually encounter problems—it's only a matter of time. Continually withdrawing from someone's bank account without making corresponding deposits quickly depletes all your interpersonal capital, and your relationship begins experiencing stress. Making people feel important and appreciating them are easy ways to make deposits into people's accounts to avoid becoming overdrawn. You can get work done *and* deposit into others' accounts at the same time by making nearly every interaction with a person a deposit. People want to be around individuals who operate this way. Be like this, and you might be surprised how many people want to associate with you. You'll be recharging their batteries, and it won't take much effort on your part.

APPRECIATION MOTIVATES PEOPLE

If you are not consciously appreciating the people around you, you're not using one of the simplest and least expensive ways to motivate people. In most cases, appreciation is free (we'll talk about some exceptions later) and is quick to administer. Saying something as simple as "Great job writing that spec. You did an outstanding job enumerating the potential problem areas" does wonders for the morale of a fellow engineer. You should be sincere when appreciating others, but that shouldn't be hard because people do many good things all day long. We just have to be on the lookout.

Always try to be specific with your appreciation. If a co-worker did a good job creating slides for a technical presentation, tell them specifically what you liked about it so that your appreciation is more personal. What would you rather hear your manager say: "Thanks for delivering that solution to the customer," or "Tom, I'm impressed with how fast you isolated the customer's problem and implemented the solution. Not many engineers on the team could have delivered on such a compressed time line. You really went above and beyond. Thank you"? Calling out something specific someone has done is much more effective than passing by them and throwing out a blanket "Good job."

Blanket appreciations are very common in the workplace. Sending an email to everyone in the company saying, "Great job, team!" is not the best way to communicate your appreciation. That impersonal message doesn't actually make anyone feel appreciated—at least not to the degree the sender is hoping. The sender's heart might be in the right place, but specific appreciation, ideally one on one, comes across as more genuine and is the best way to acknowledge something someone has done. Make the effort to find out who had a major role in whatever milestone was achieved and go thank those people in person. It requires more time, but it's an infinitely more powerful form of appreciation.

No one likes to work tirelessly, year after year, and never receive any recognition. No one. Even engineers who seem to be driven by the thrill of their technologies need to hear words of appreciation and encouragement on a consistent basis. It's food for their souls. Don't starve the people around you by never appreciating them.

It's very hard for anyone to give all day long and have no one acknowledge it. If you feel unappreciated, be the person to sow that first seed with one of your fellow engineers. Someone has to get the ship moving in the right direction—it may as well be you. Appreciate the people you work with more, and things will start working better. At a minimum, your time spent together will be more enjoyable.

If you are in a high-level leadership position in your organization, don't underestimate the power your appreciation has on motivating the people under you, especially the ones doing the real hands-on work. You may be missing out daily on the opportunity to motivate others with simple words of appreciation. In general, people look up to you and give a lot of weight to what you say. If you talk to them about something praiseworthy that they are doing for their team, you validate them as a person and as an engineer. Everybody likes that.

The appreciation you give costs you nothing, so what are you waiting for? You already know people are figuratively starving for it, so hand it out as fast and as often as possible. Deciding to honestly and frequently appreciate people is like providing a food aid program to a starving country. People are hungry for what we have. The difference between you and a relief program is that you'll never run out of food. You can keep on giving and giving. You know people want it. You know you have it. Use the power of appreciation to show people they are valued and motivate people to do bigger and better things.

APPRECIATION SHOULD BE A LIFESTYLE

While occasionally appreciating people and making them feel important is a good start, the goal is to make these activities a habit that becomes a part of your everyday life. Similar to the cliché example of lifting weights, if you want true, long-lasting change, you must hit the gym more than just a couple of times a year. When it comes to forming good habits, you'll probably have to continually remind yourself to do the right things at first, but after a few short weeks, you'll start doing them without thinking.

A culture of appreciation should be at the core of your teams. Why waste time taking people for granted and ignoring their contributions when it takes so little to keep their gas tanks full? If you don't currently encourage those around you, you probably don't understand how powerful this simple act can be. Mary Kay Ash, founder of Mary Kay Cosmetics, said, "Everyone has an invisible sign hanging from his neck saying, 'Make me feel important.'" Everyone wants to feel like they are doing something that matters. Everyone wants to feel connected to something larger than themselves. One way to help people feel connected is to help them feel important, because they *are* important.

If you're the type of person who doesn't regularly appreciate the people around you, you're missing out on a huge opportunity. You may feel uncomfortable interacting with people, but you're going to have to make a decision: Do you want the results of appreciation in your organization or not? Do you want to work in a happier, better connected environment or not? Wanting, wishing, and hoping does not bring about real change, only action does.

Here's an easy solution to help you: *Make* yourself appreciate people. Put systems in place that you can follow to help you do the things you know you should be doing. Work with a buddy to help each other grow in this area. Put reminders in your phone or email calendar. A simple calendar reminder could prompt you to appreciate someone on your team at 3:00 p.m., making it an easy and effective way to force yourself to do what you already know is right. After you start seeing the results, you'll become more motivated to keep up with it without needing the reminder.

TANGIBLE GIFTS

Would you rather hear someone say that you've done a good job, or come back to your workspace and find a handwritten note of appreciation attached to a gift card to your favorite coffee shop? People, in general, really like getting gifts regardless of their age, income bracket, or gender. Use this knowledge of human nature to more effectively recognize the contributions of the people around you.

Tangible gifts mean a lot to people because someone took the time and spent the money to put them together. In a money-obsessed world, the person who actively finds ways to give it away instantly separates themselves from everyone else. You operate at a higher level than most people, which gives you an advantage as you attempt to become more influential and helpful with those around you.

With very little effort, I could tell you what's most important to you. Do you want to know how? I'd just follow you around for a week and see where you spend your time and money. If you say you truly value people but don't spend your time or money helping them, appreciating them, or making them feel important, then you're lying to yourself. It's like saying golf is very important to you, but you don't own a set of golf clubs and haven't golfed in the past ten years. Maybe it *used to* be important to you, but it isn't anymore. If you don't spend any time or money on an activity, organization, or person, then it's not that important to you. You may acknowledge the importance of it, but unless you're personally invested in it via time or money, your actions prove it isn't that important to you personally. I have called this the Universal Importance Test, or UIT for short.

If all your money is tied up in the stock market, the stock market becomes very important to you. If you spend all your money on your car, your car is very important to you. If the local homeless shelter is important to you, you volunteer there or donate resources to it. If you never spend time appreciating people, developing them, making them feel important, or giving to them, then according to the UIT, they aren't important to you.

I recently joined a new development team where I work. Joining a new team, especially one that has a completely different technology stack than you're used to, can be difficult. There is a lot to learn, not only about the technologies being used, but about how and why things work the way they do. Regardless of past experiences, someone moving to a new team needs a lot of help in the beginning to learn the idiosyncrasies of how development is accomplished. I was no different when transitioning to the new team.

I'm always painfully aware of how much time and energy I'm syphoning from the other engineers on my team. I try to keep tabs on our mutual bank accounts and I want to make sure I'm not withdrawing too much. If I do feel like I've been asking too much from a specific engineer, it's not uncommon for me to verbally thank them for what they've done but also follow up the appreciation with a tangible gift of some sort.

On one occasion, I felt like I'd been haunting another engineer on my team because of his expertise in a particular area. After the deliverable was wrapped up, I ordered a video game we had talked about a few times in the past and wrapped it like a present. When I gave it to him, I told him how much I appreciated his help, and I wanted to show it in a tangible way. I could tell he was totally caught off guard, in a good way. The gift *showed* him how important his help was to me because I spent my resources of time and money appreciating him. My appreciation of him passed the UIT.

Not all appreciation needs to be demonstrated with a tangible gift; but in the cases that warrant it, do it. Put the idea in your interpersonal tool box. It's one of the strongest forms of appreciation available, and it goes a long way in recognizing the contributions of the people you work with.

INITIATE INTERACTIONS WITH PEOPLE

Introverts are probably squirming in their seats because this section is about why we should proactively seek opportunities to interact with people and build stronger relationships. We need to see the importance of getting out of our seats and getting to know more about the people we work with.

Initiating interactions with people makes them feel important, especially if you are in any position of leadership in your organization. People know that you have limited time and resources, so when you spend some of it on them, it shows them that they are important to you (UIT). It's good to remember that if your words and your actions disagree, people will always believe your actions. You can say people are important, but if you never talk to them and get to know them, your actions are telling them they're not *that* important.

People in leadership positions, whether technical or management, need to make time to get out and talk with other managers and engineers. Setting aside only thirty minutes each week to contact one new engineer in your organization would allow you to talk to more than fifty people in a single year. For some senior leaders, this may be their entire group. If you work for a larger company, that might be only a small amount of the organization, but so what? It's fifty real, breathing people you could encourage and appreciate. It shouldn't be a time thing; it should be an importance thing. You can get as creative as you want to in this space. Hold a get-together where you invite a half-dozen people to a free pizza lunch once a month. The issue isn't really what you're doing as a group, but that you're connecting with individuals to deposit into their bank accounts.

The only way to significantly build stronger relationships with people is by spending time with them. If you doubt this, try moving to a different city and see how the relationships with your current friends and family fare. At best, they'll stagnate. Typically, those relationships deteriorate because you're not spending the necessary time with each other anymore. That's why long-distance relationships seldom work out. People begin growing roots in a new location and feel closer to those directly around them. No amount of emailing or texting can make up for this physical separation.

Do you feel disconnected at work? If so, start spending more time with your co-workers. You'll begin feeling more connected to them. Do you feel anxiety because your company is growing, and you prefer smaller teams? Get to know the new people better. You might not get to know everybody, but the more people you do know, the more connected you'll feel with the change that's taking place. You have a part to play in how connected you are to anything or anybody. If you feel like an outsider, kick down the imaginary door and get inside!

Initiating interactions with other people comes easier for some of us than others, but everyone can get better at it. Even though you think you're not good with people, all you need is a little practice and some go-to tools to help you in situations that make you feel uncomfortable. Don't let fear limit your interaction with others. Often, we'll need to be the ones who approach other people and says words of encouragement or recognize a contribution they've made. If we don't do it, it may never happen.

SUMMARY

- People are chronically underappreciated and crave appreciation.

- Appreciation is one of the easiest ways to keep people motivated.

- Make appreciation a habit in your life—it should become part of your core character.

- You spend your time and money on what's most important to you (Universal Importance Test).

- People, regardless of background, like tangible gifts. If you want to take your appreciation to the next level and it's warranted, appreciate people in a tangible way.

- You shouldn't expect people to come to you. Instead, you'll need to initiate interactions with them to show them they are important to you.

- Make time to interact with others, especially if you are in any sort of leadership position.

CHAPTER 9

Get to Know Others

How many times have you met a person whom, on first impression you didn't particularly like, but later you ended up making into a friend? This has happened to me several times over the past few years. What was the breakthrough in each instance? Spending small amounts of time together with the intention of getting to know more about each other. Not everyone is easy to get to know. Some people create a shell around them to protect themselves from others. They may have been mistreated in the past, or maybe they're naturally standoffish. On the surface, they seem cold and aloof, but inside, they are nice, funny, and interesting. A little extra effort can be needed to penetrate their shell.

I worked with an engineer who was 100 percent business as usual on the surface. He didn't go out of his way to talk with people, and he put off a leave-me-alone kind of vibe. He was a fantastic employee; he just didn't possess a bubbly sort of personality. I made it my personal goal to get to know him better because I find these types of people often become some of my most rewarding relationships.

Over the course of several months, I took every opportunity to find out more about him. While getting coffee in the break room one day, I found out he served in the military. We instantly bonded over our common experience of military service. I also found out that he was a huge fan of music like I am. We started sharing what we thought about different bands. What was the outcome of all of this? He became one of my favorite people at work. He's funny, interesting, and a joy to be around. He's great! Had I given up early in the process and not taken the time to get to know him, I would have missed out on a friendship that has increased my quality of life at work.

WHAT'S IMPORTANT TO THEM?

When getting to know more about the people around us, remember the goal is to find out more about *them*, not to cram all our personal exploits down their throats. People most enjoy talking about their own interests and desires. Let them do that, at least in the early stages of getting to know more about them. Find out what they're passionate about and give them a platform to share that passion. You may end up talking about work-related topics at first, but given enough time, the conversation will progress to more interesting topics. Times like these are important because you get to look behind the carefully constructed curtain and see who they truly are.

Asking a third party about someone else on your team can be a useful tactic when trying to find out more about a person. You can then use this information to kick-start some of your conversations later down the road. For example, ask your manager or a co-worker what kinds of activities your fellow engineer likes. If you find out your team member likes to mountain bike, you can use this information when you strike up a conversation with him or her in the future. If they're like most people, they'll go on and on about mountain biking because it's something that genuinely interests them. This approach gives you an easy gateway into conversations that are not strictly work-related.

People feel connected to others when they understand them on a deeper level. If you take the time to get to know others in a more meaningful way than the occasional short, impersonal greeting as you walk past each other, you'll strengthen your connections with the people around you. These important connections facilitate the free flow of information between individuals and contribute to a more inclusive work environment and increased psychological safety.

MAKE YOURSELF AVAILABLE

If you look like you don't want to talk to people, people will avoid interacting with you. If you never go to where people are, you'll miss out on opportunities to get to know them. You can't hole up in your office or cube all day long and expect to have any sort of meaningful interactions with people. There are numerous opportunities to interact with others every day. Make it a point to interact with people, not just for your sake but for theirs as well. People want to be connected to others in their organization. It makes them feel happier and safer.

Many businesses have common areas where employees tend to linger. Some offices have a break room where employees can gather, or they have a common area by the microwave and coffee machines. People go there to get snacks, heat up their lunches, and most importantly, get coffee! Places like this are ideal spots to converse with people we may not normally interact with.

Common areas are great because you know which times people flock to them. If you're willing to get to know people better, use these locations to your advantage. Drop by at lunch when people use the microwaves to heat up their food. Strike up a conversation with someone who is waiting two to three minutes for a frozen burrito to warm up. The person isn't doing anything better anyway, so you aren't interrupting their work, if that's a concern of yours.

Meetings and events at the office are also good opportunities to get better acquainted with people. Show up early and use those few minutes to talk about something outside of work. It may sound like a revolutionary idea, but you're totally allowed to come to a meeting early if you want to. Take these extra few minutes to talk with people who you'd never normally get a chance to speak to. It's an easy way to get to know more people, and all you do is show up to your planned meeting a few minutes early. You've wasted an opportunity if you show up right when the meeting starts.

Little time is required to significantly increase the frequency and quality of your interactions with people. You don't have to set aside an additional two hours of your day to do this. Spend ten minutes more going to people instead of making them come to you. A lot of engineers may never seek you out, so you must go to them. That's just the way it is. If you want to foster a connected environment in your organization, you're the one who's going to have to make it happen with some people.

Generally, people in technical leadership positions are completely in the other ditch, and *never* come by for casual conversation with the intent of getting to know you better. If you're in any kind of leadership position in your organization, you don't have to wait for a handwritten invitation to connect with other engineers—just go do it! Force yourself to go connect with others, even if it doesn't come naturally. People would love to talk with you as long as you don't continually violate the principles in this book. Don't assume that you're bothering them. Instead, you're making yourself available.

IF YOU WANT TO BE LIKED, BE LIKEABLE

If we want more mutually beneficial connections to the people around us, we'll need to exhibit the qualities those individuals are looking for. We can't be frustrated because no one "gets us," then turn around and be critical, impatient, and intolerant of everyone we interact with. The people around us pick up those signals loud and clear. Our actions are saying "messing with me is bad news." They'll avoid interacting with us.

Have you ever been around a house cat that is having a bad day and wants to be left alone? Typically, he isolates himself, slicks back his ears when approached, and hisses. The message the cat is sending is unmistakable: Leave me alone or I'll inflict pain on you. Many people behave the same way in their personal and professional lives and then wonder why things aren't working out for them socially. If you're figuratively behaving like the cat in the illustration, people will steer clear of you—they don't want to get scratched.

Over the past sixteen years, I've known numerous engineers who behaved like the cat in the previous example. Whenever I saw them, they were never smiling. At meetings, they were always critical of other engineers and managers. Anytime I needed to interact with them, they acted like their sole objective was to get the conversation over with as fast as possible. My attitude toward them became: "I get it kitty, you don't want to be bothered. I'll leave you alone." The signals they were sending were unmistakable.

Simply put, if you want to be liked, be more likeable. The more supportive, appreciative, and helpful you are to others, the more people want to be associated with you. It makes intuitive sense because human beings naturally want to be around others that add value to them in some way.

If each person took personal ownership of doing the right thing in all their interactions, corporate propaganda wouldn't be needed to promote culture. Management cannot dictate the quality of our interpersonal interactions any more than the government can dictate morals. Laws are only effective as long as someone is watching and enforcing them.

Companies are their people. They need grassroots change when it comes to a connected work environment, and that only happens when individuals take personal responsibility for their connections to their co-workers. Your organization will become an awesome place to come to every day when its people do the necessary actions to make it healthy from a people perspective.

You disqualify yourself from complaining about your work environment if you don't do your part to promote its health from a people perspective. You can't say you want the benefits of a great work environment and then literally do nothing to *make* it better. Operating this way is symptomatic of not realizing how important interpersonal connections are to the health of your teams.

THE POWER OF LUNCH

Everyone has to eat. Why not use this fact to your advantage in order to learn more about the engineers you work with? To build out your Opportunity Tree, start inviting people to lunch on a regular basis and pay for it yourself, if the other person will allow it. This accomplishes a couple of things:

1. It shows them they are important.
2. Because you're buying, it doesn't put any sort of burden on them. All they have to do is show up and get a free meal. People rarely say no to a free lunch.

How many times in the last year has someone offered you a free lunch just to get to know you better? Your answer may be zero. Why is this? It could be because of money, but it also could be because it never crosses other people's minds to use lunch as an opportunity to connect with you. You don't have to take someone to a four-star restaurant. A delicious burrito from a local food truck is just as effective if the intent is to spend more one-on-one time with a person. The time, effort, and money you spend do not go unnoticed by the person you've invited to join you for lunch. It's another tangible way to deposit into their interpersonal bank account.

Lunch is great because it's a solid thirty minutes to an hour of one-on-one communication, which we already know is the primary way to strengthen a relationship. You can undo years of weird interactions just by going out to eat with them one time. Buying someone lunch is almost like a magic cure-all. It instantly changes the dynamic of your relationship with that person, especially if the two of you have never spent any time outside of work before. Don't pass up this easy way to strengthen a connection with someone.

Lunch provides an opportunity to engage in relaxed conversation. People don't feel compelled to get back to their workspace while they are eating, so they are more open to talking about things that aren't related to work. That's what allows us to get to know them better. When you pluck them out of work and put them into a more casual environment, you might be surprised at how much they open up about their hobbies and interests, which is mutually beneficial.

The point of this chapter is to emphasize that it's *our* responsibility to connect with the people around us, not theirs. Making our organization a better place to work is not only the responsibility of the people in positions of authority, it's everyone's responsibility. Leaders can create a framework and support the activities, but at the end of the day, everyone in the organization needs to do the things that will ensure others feel connected and valued. This doesn't happen by accident. It happens by doing all the little things we know to do, day after day, in all our interactions. Proactively connect with people because if you're waiting for them to do it, it's most likely not going to happen.

SUMMARY

- Some people require extra effort when you are trying to get to know them better. Don't give up.

- Everyone has things they are passionate about outside of work. Find out what those are with the people around you.

- If you look like you don't want to talk to people, others will avoid you.

- Set some time aside to get to know people better. Just ten minutes a day can go a long way toward building a healthier people environment.

- Exhibiting the traits of a likeable person is attractive to others. Always be aware of the signs you are displaying to those around you.

- Invite people to lunch to spend time outside of work with them. It doesn't have to be anything fancy—it's the conversation that's important.

- It's *your* job to make your company the best place to work. You may not be able to directly affect monetary compensation, but you can definitely affect the work environment.

CHAPTER 10

Names. Yup, They're That Important

The concept in this chapter has been one of the most fruitful for me personally from a people-skills perspective. It's surprising how much of a positive impact you can make on others by simply remembering their names. It sounds trivial, but its effect is quite profound. You can turn a cold work environment into a warm, lively atmosphere by doing nothing more than remembering names and using them in your normal day-to-day interactions.

Remembering people's names instantly separates you from others. Instead of being one of the dozens of people others casually pass by each day while looking at the ground, you become someone who *knows* them. You may not know them in any significant way yet, but learning their names is the first step in that process. Names are the bridge into more meaningful conversations—it's one of the first steps to more interesting interactions. Names immediately break down barriers with people you don't talk with very often and create an atmosphere in which you can learn a little more about them.

There is no reason you have to keep seeing the same people day after day without learning their names. I acknowledge that meeting new people can sometimes be uncomfortable, but you know what's even more uncomfortable than asking someone their name? Seeing them a few times a day around the office and refusing to find out who they are. Instead of saying "hey," you will be able to say, "How's it going, William?" Who knows where the conversation will lead after that.

You might be surprised by how many engineers will completely ignore you, won't even talk to you or look you in the eyes, until you learn their names. Engineers can spend years not talking to others they work around just because they didn't bother to learn their names. Be the initiator. Learn people's names and make your work environment a little less awkward for everyone. If you want to get better interacting with people, this is one of the most foundational principles there is.

JUST ASK

I have never had someone refuse to give me their name when I asked. That's right, never. Even complete strangers I've never seen before have no problem giving me their names. I don't have some special power over people, either. I just ask.

Stop avoiding people and come right out and ask them their names. It saves you a lot of awkward conversations in the future. You don't need to use a fancy, super witty, or funny approach. Just ask. Tell them you see them around all the time, but you don't know their name. Let them tell you what it is. It works every single time. If you're worried about someone rejecting you, don't be.

I constantly hear people say things like: "I've been working here a year and see that girl every day, and I don't know her name. We even occasionally talk to each other." This is easy to fix. Just ask her what her name is.

Proactively asking people their names saves you from embarrassment later when you're in a situation where the other person realizes you don't know their name and you should. Situations like this can occur when you least expect them, such as when you are introducing people and you can't identify the person you've been talking to for the past year. This can be uncomfortable for you, and it also demonstrates to the person, whose name you didn't bother to learn, that they weren't important enough to you to learn who they are.

DEMONSTRATE PEOPLE ARE IMPORTANT TO YOU

If someone tells you their name and you forget it, they'll probably give you a break the next time you see them. However, if you continue to forget it, the message you're sending is clear: They're not important enough to remember their name. Ouch.

After I started working at a new company, I was walking by the main door to our floor and saw our CEO approaching on his little scooter (he had hurt his leg). Like a good corporate citizen, I rushed to open the door for him, so he wouldn't have to figure out how to get his scooter through while at the same time propping the door open. When I opened the door, he said something to me that forever changed my opinion of him as a person. He said, "Thank you, Tony." I was completely caught off guard. He knew my name! He knew who I was! I didn't remember telling him who I was, but he somehow knew it. It may seem like a small thing, but it profoundly affected me. Never underestimate the power of knowing and using someone's name, especially if you are in a position of leadership in your organization.

Remembering people's names demonstrates they're important to you. In a very general way, a name represents the person as a whole. When you use people's names, you address them as individuals and show them they're not expendable employees. At the very least, it demonstrates to the individual that they are important enough to deserve a permanent place in your memory banks. Don't underestimate how important this can be to those around you.

NAMES PERSONALIZE INTERACTIONS

Names are so important to people that you should find ways to incorporate them into your everyday interactions. Whenever possible, and in any sort of interaction, try to squeeze in the individual's name. You may think this would cause your interactions to seem unnatural, but it doesn't. You can easily personalize all your interactions using simple techniques like these.

When you pass by someone at work, use their name. Instead of ignoring the person or giving them an impersonal greeting, call them by name. You accomplish three things by doing this:

1. You show that you remember their name, which may not be a big deal for people you've known a long time, but it is important to people you rarely talk to.
2. If you say it with a smile, it's a nice way to brighten up someone's day.
3. It personalizes the interaction.

Whenever possible, use names. Don't be weird about it and try to say the name an unnatural amount of times, but think about how you could use it more often. It's typically very easy to either start or finish an interaction with a name, so don't miss those opportunities. If you meet with Susan to discuss a project, start the conversation with, "Thanks for meeting with me, Susan," and finish the conversation by saying, "Thanks for helping, Susan." Rather than then a generic "thanks," you have personalized the conversation by using her name.

These suggestions may seem trivial to some people, but things like this are what separate those who are good with people from those who are not. If you develop good habits in all your small interactions, the big ones will be much easier to navigate because you've already gained a small amount of influence and goodwill with the people around you. Don't think that becoming more skillful with people is just about successfully handling the big interactions such as consoling a person when a loved one passes away. It's not. It's about consistently doing all the little things you know to do every day, whether you feel like it or not.

THE MILLION-DOLLAR TEST

Say you and I were in a room, and I announced that I had a little test for you. I sat you down in a chair and brought in ten complete strangers and lined them up in front of you. I explain that each one of these people will take turns saying his or her name one time. The next day, we'll all come back into this room, and if you can give me their names, I'll give you one million dollars. You can use whatever you want to help you remember their names. Do you think you could do it? Of course you could! Why? Because now it's important to you. You might use your smartphone, write the names down on paper, etch them on the wall with a piece of metal, or anything else you could think of.

It's not that you can't remember names. It's that you never learned that remembering people's names is one of the easiest ways to gain positive influence with others, and it costs you nothing.

I work with software engineering savants that can rattle off arcane multiline Bash shell commands they used only one time ten years ago but can't remember the name of an electrical engineer that works three rows down that they see every day. Really? How is that possible? It's because they haven't yet learned how important names are to people and the positive effect remembering them can have on others.

Some people are probably thinking they work with too many people to remember all their names. It's a common excuse, especially if you work for anything bigger than a start-up. Don't give up, though. Start small and expand into other teams. You already know the names of the people you work with every day. What about the teams you *associate* with occasionally? Pick a team and learn the names of everyone on it. When you have those names down, move to the next team and learn those. It's much easier than it sounds because you're learning only a handful of names at a time.

This may sound like something a stalker would do, but another tactic you can use is to pull up the organizational chart (the chart with names and images of company employees) for other teams and learn names that way. When you see the individuals from that team around the office, you already know their names. Your time in the office is much more enjoyable when you know more about those you work with.

Changing your behavior when it comes to learning names may be an absolute game changer for you. If you're looking for a quick way to jump-start more meaningful interactions with others, learning names would be a very good way to start.

TIPS FOR REMEMBERING MORE NAMES

When I'm in a situation where I need to remember people's names, I consciously put myself into a different mindset. For example, when I'm at a restaurant, I tell myself to pay attention when the waiter introduces himself to us. I put myself into a name-remembering zone. Because it's important to me that I remember his name, I make it a big deal and, as a result, I'm now much better at remembering names than I used to be.

My family and I frequent a restaurant where I use this tactic with great results. Every time we show up, the place turns into a party. People start talking to us, asking how things are going. The manager asks about things we talked about during our last visit. Waitresses stop by our table just to talk. I feel like we get the A+ treatment for no other reason than we learned and remember their names.

Another approach I have used at work is to keep a list of people's names at my desk. Whenever I meet someone new and think I may have trouble remembering their name, I immediately write it down when I get back to my desk. Periodically, I'll review the list to make sure I haven't forgotten any names. It's simple to do, and I need my list far less than I first thought I would.

When you meet someone for the first time and they tell you their name, try to associate the name with something or someone else with the same name. Your brain is good at that. When you see the person the next time, instead of trying to recall their name, your brain will bring the association back to you with the correct name attached. For example, if someone tells me his name is Luke, I'll associate his face with Luke Skywalker from the *Star Wars* movies. Remembering his name is much easier after that. I use this approach all the time and find it very helpful.

If someone tells you their name, and you can't hear it or its pronunciation is difficult, ask the person to repeat it. The person won't think less of you for that. Actually, the opposite will occur. The person will think *more* of you because you want to make sure you heard the name correctly—it was important to you. You may even have to ask the person to spell the name if it's unique. Do whatever it takes.

As engineers, we work in fields where it is not uncommon to meet people from different parts of the world. Some of these people have names that are difficult to pronounce. As a result, you may have to ask someone to repeat their name several times before you're able to pronounce it correctly. That's OK. Alternatively, you can also ask them to spell out their name to aid in pronunciation. Do whatever is necessary to make sure you know their name the next time you meet or talk on the phone. They know they're in a different country and their name is more unusual than what is typically found in this country. They will happily assist you in learning their name and greatly appreciate the additional effort you put in to do so.

Don't tell yourself that you're bad at remembering names. If you say you're bad at remembering names, you won't put forth the required effort to learn them. Because you've already decided you can't, you've given yourself an out. Having justified your lack of trying, you don't give yourself a chance to get better. Instead, continually remind yourself that you're getting better at remembering names and make it a priority to do so.

SUMMARY

- Remembering people's names is one of the easiest and most profound ways to make a positive impact on a person's perception of us.

- Stop ignoring people and just ask them their names. Don't worry about being rejected. You won't be.

- Show people they're important to you by remembering their names. If you are in a position of leadership at your workplace, remembering names has an even more profound effect on people.

- Use people's names whenever possible to personalize interactions.

- Change your view on remembering names by realizing how important they are to the individual. Don't treat people like cogs. Treat them like the unique individuals they are. Remembering a person's name demonstrates the importance of someone.

- Don't make excuses for not being able to remember names. You're an engineer; you can remember whatever you deem important.

> Employ whatever tactics are necessary to aid in remembering names. If you have to, put people's names into your phone or write them down at your desk.

CHAPTER 11
How to Correct People

At some point in your career, you'll run into a situation where you have to correct another engineer. It's unavoidable and should be viewed as a necessary part of a healthy growing team. Engineers *should* continually sharpen each other by pointing out better ways to get work done. Correction, administered properly, can help a person change their behavior to get better results *and* strengthen interpersonal connections at the same time —it's actually a good thing. Many engineers seem to get tripped up because they use very few proven methods when administering correction, which results in unnecessary friction between themselves and the person they are attempting to correct.

This chapter presents a handful of strategies you can use the next time you find it necessary to correct someone. These strategies can be used on anyone in your life, not just other engineers. As an example, if you have children, you can use these same approaches on them, too. It can be tough some days because our kids seem to know the quickest ways to get under our skin, but we shouldn't let that stop us from doing what's right. If they don't learn the correct behaviors from us, they'll most likely learn them from others who don't have their best interests at heart. If we can do the things in this book with our families, we can do them with anyone. Use your friends and family members as your test subjects.

DOES IT MATTER IF THEY ARE WRONG?

If you think you need to correct someone, the first thing you should ask yourself is this: Does it *really* matter if the person is wrong? Is something important at stake if you don't correct the individual? This isn't the case nearly as often as some engineers' behavior seems to warrant. The error, which just *has to* be corrected, may not even be relevant.

Many times, people act like the self-proclaimed "word police" and feel it's their duty to correct every syllable of every word that comes out of someone's mouth. There are also fact-checkers who must make sure every single statement is 100 percent, verifiably true. If it's not, they have to address that issue before moving on. People don't like this, and if you operate this way, it wears on those around you.

My grandparents, who have both passed away, were a perfect example of this playing out in real life. During my visits with them in their later years, my grandfather would be telling me a story, and my grandmother would interject herself into the conversation a couple times each sentence to correct some fact or figure she thought my grandfather had stated incorrectly. Instead of catching a 40-pound salmon in Alaska, it was 42 pounds. Instead of seeing a grizzly bear with her three cubs, it was two cubs. My grandmother didn't understand that the details weren't important. They were irrelevant to the purpose of the stories, which were to relate the impressive things my grandfather saw or did on one of his trips to Alaska. Not only was this exhausting to listen to, it must have been frustrating from my grandfather's standpoint.

Dave Hendricksen, author of the book *12 Essential Skills for Software Architects,* said, "One of the first principles to learn in becoming a gracious professional is to choose relationships over correctness." This is a powerful statement and one that has stuck with me since I first read his book years ago. Is it more important to correct a person or to keep their goodwill? Depending on how you go about administering the correction and how often you do it, you could be making frequent, large withdrawals out of a person's interpersonal bank account and risking going in the red. Ask yourself whether it's more important to correct the person or to cultivate a stronger connection to the individual.

There's a time and a place for detailed discussions, but being overly detailed across the board slows down progress and is not necessary, especially in strategic conversations. Many times, it's sufficient to be generally correct to move a discussion along.

Some engineers will completely withdraw and stop participating in meetings because they get tired of having every word that comes out of their mouth overanalyzed. No one wants to continually have their input put through the ringer in front of everyone else. An environment like this shuts down creativity. This behavior is bad for team effectiveness because the more engineers who are wholeheartedly participating, the more productive your time together will be. Don't let someone put a damper on that by being overly critical at the wrong time.

Your goal is to create the safest, most supportive atmosphere you can within your team. If you constantly correct everyone's words and statements, especially on details that are irrelevant at the time, you cause people to stop participating—it makes them feel bad about themselves. Instead of brainstorming with you on a possible solution to a problem, they are more concerned with speaking perfectly, which significantly limits the quality of thinking you're getting out of them. If you want the best out of people, they need to feel empowered to share what's on their mind, regardless of how unpolished the idea or comment may be.

I occasionally lead brainstorming sessions as part of my job. When I lead these sessions, the first idea I write on the whiteboard is "time machine." It sounds silly, but I do this to let everyone know that anything short of traveling back and forth in time is an acceptable idea. It lightens the mood in the room and lets people know they are in a safe environment. People typically will offer their ideas least likely to be rejected first. If you show them they're in a safe environment, and no one is waiting to attack their ideas, they'll start to bring out their really good ideas, the ideas that might transform your business. Don't hamper the ideation process by being overly critical at the wrong time.

CORRECT PEOPLE IN PRIVATE, IF POSSIBLE

When you find yourself in a situation where you do need to administer any sort of significant correction, the best way to do it is in private. No one likes to have his or her faults or shortcomings paraded out in front of everyone. Making corrections in private allows people to save face among their fellow co-workers and will take some of the inevitable defensiveness out of the air because they don't have to stand up for themselves to the degree that they would in a public setting. Correcting people in private should be viewed as a common courtesy.

People are social creatures and anything that threatens their social standing is viewed as an attack, especially if you don't have strong relationships with them to begin with. Engineers have a lot of knowledge and technical ability, but they can be sensitive when their work is being corrected by others. This is another reason why building up your bank accounts with people can be so helpful. Some types of corrections can be *huge* withdrawals. Improperly handled public corrections may completely empty another person's bank account—so watch out!

Engineers are valued for their knowledge and technical ability. One-upping others can be very tempting in the moment because it can give you an ego boost to show everyone how capable you are. Watch out! These are the kinds of behaviors that cause relational problems between people and different parts of organizations. Part of maturing as an engineer is understanding not only the technical minutiae of your job, but also the dynamics between individuals and groups of people.

Resist the urge to drag people down publicly, because it's typically unhelpful, and it also has negative consequences associated with it that can adversely affect future communication and morale.

Despite your best efforts, you may face instances where you cannot avoid correcting someone in a public setting. In situations like this, be mindful of the other person and frame the correction in the best way possible.

Say you are in a meeting room with six other engineers going over the design for a key piece of technology that will be included in an upcoming product. While listening to a junior engineer go through her design proposal, you notice some glaring omissions that will need to be addressed before your team can begin implementing the feature. Chances are you're not the only one who noticed the omissions. What do you do? For starters, you can acknowledge the deficiencies by saying something like: "I noticed there are a few key cases missing in your proposal. They are X, Y, and Z. I'd be happy to work with you on those after this meeting if nobody here has a problem with that." In essence, you're telling her you see a problem and instead of adding insult to injury, you're offering to help her fix it. Operating this way can help minimize embarrassment and can keep further faultfinding from ensuing. Tactics like this allow people to save face and build trust while being corrected. A win-win situation.

Sometimes it can be helpful to think of life like a marathon rather than a sprint. In our quest to be fast, thorough, and impressive to our peers and superiors (by sprinting), are we affecting our performance later in the race? Sure, at mile two we may be looking really good, but what about at mile twenty? Will we still have as much goodwill and influence with the people around us, or will we have spent all of it in our quest to stand out using tactics with known bad side effects? Decide to correct people in a way that not only works for you in the short term but also ensures you're in a good position toward the end of the race, too.

FOCUS ON THE BEHAVIOR, NOT THE PERSON

People receive your correction much better if you keep it impersonal. Always focus on the behavior that isn't meeting the standard, and not the person. If you focus on the person, your correction will be more damaging because it is a direct blow against the individual. Correction should never be a personal attack.

When I played guitar for a local volunteer organization, we had three teams of musicians, and I was the leader of one of the teams. When we rehearsed, there were endless opportunities to put this principle into practice.

One of my major responsibilities was to make sure the music we played sounded as good and as professional as possible. This required a fair amount of public correction on my part to make sure we played the songs correctly and we all sounded good together. Public correction was unavoidable because of the nature of the setting. It wasn't feasible to pull people aside, in private, to address execution issues during practice. This would have taken way too long, and the other musicians needed to hear the correction, so they could apply it to their own instruments, if needed. I had to get really good at administering correction with other people present.

If something didn't sound right while we practiced a song, I'd wait for the song to finish or stop it right then, whichever was warranted. I'd ask questions to lead the other musicians to the problem. I would say something like, "I'm not sure that part during the verse sounded right, what do you think?" Do you see how this is different than, "You played that part wrong"? The first correction is focused on the part being played. The second correction is focused on the individual. The difference may seem subtle to you, but it means a lot to the person receiving the correction, especially in front of other people.

Like musicians, engineers are also an interesting breed of people. It takes special care to guide and grow them without offending them or wounding their technical and creative spirits. For some of these people, their work is almost sacred to them, and they view it as an extension of themselves. To get the best out of your people, you need to become as smooth as butter at correcting and guiding them.

CUSHION THE BLOW

The key to getting the results you want while keeping the goodwill of the person you're correcting is all about your approach. This section has a couple of concrete tools you can use to cushion the blow when you find you have to correct someone.

At this point, you've already pulled the person aside and created a safe environment to administer the correction. Ideally, you already have a healthy interpersonal bank account with the individual, but even if you don't, these strategies are still effective. Don't go into a discussion like this unprepared. Know what you plan to say, and what tools you plan to apply. Predetermine your game plan and stick to it. There is no reason to fly by the seat of your pants and awkwardly stumble through the conversation which would make it even more uncomfortable than it already might be for the both of you.

A common technique for administering correction is called the sandwich method. The idea here is that you start and end with something positive and sandwich the correction in between the two. The positive remarks don't have to be over-the-top and shouldn't be any form of excessive or insincere praise. If you were going to perform surgery on someone, you'd give the patient painkillers first. All you're trying to do here is numb the pain a little before you pull out your scalpel and go to work.

Some have expressed concern that using this method will mask the real issue, so a person only hears the positive remarks and misses the correction. I don't think I've ever seen it work out that way, but perhaps you could be so overly positive with the ends of the sandwich that the person doesn't think anything needs to change. Starting and ending with something positive should not be a thirty-minute-long exposition on how the individual is a credit to humanity and that anyone with half a brain would be lucky to have them working on their team. Say something short and sweet to help dull the upcoming pain. Start out by saying you were impressed with the work they did on project X, if it's true. Or, say something about how you appreciate their punctuality, if they are. You should never lie, and you should keep it to a reasonable length.

This isn't about applying an unchangeable set of rules. If you find a person isn't responding to your method of correction, try adjusting your approach. If you find something doesn't work for you, tweak it a little the next time around. You get better at correcting people the more you do it. Don't give up on the idea because you tried it once, and it didn't work. Maybe you need a little more practice.

Talking about your own personal struggles is another strategy that cushions the blow when you are correcting people. This communicates to that person that you are authentic. You know you're not perfect, and you don't expect others to be perfect either. Everybody makes mistakes sometimes. The goal is to make fewer and fewer mistakes, but when someone is starting out, they are going to need a lot of correction. Even seasoned vets occasionally make mistakes and beginning the conversation with a story of personal struggle can be effective. Sharing something you had a difficult time doing will go a long way in taking some of the defensiveness out of the air.

Don't assume everyone is like you. Some people want others to give it to them straight. That might be fine for you, but the people you work with are not you. It's safer to assume everyone could be offended and then change your approach after you get to know the individuals better. If you take the bull-in-a-china-shop approach, you might create even more problems for yourself down the road.

As this chapter concludes, here are the three concrete strategies we covered that you can use when correcting people:

1. Correct people in private, if possible.
2. Focus on the behavior, not the person.
3. Cushion the blow.

Remember, how you administer correction affects how well the correction is received and how much goodwill you'll keep after the correction is over. There is a huge difference between public confrontation and ridicule and pulling someone aside and using the sandwich method on them. The first approach has the potential for creating strife between individuals; the second has the potential for continued goodwill between you and the individual being corrected. Creating an encouraging and enjoyable work environment is all about placing importance on doing the day-to-day tasks of human interaction to the best of your ability. There are no off days when it comes to interpersonal interactions.

SUMMARY

➤ Correcting someone can be uncomfortable, but if done correctly, you can get the desired results and keep your relationship intact.

➤ Before correcting someone, first decide if the offense even warrants correction. If not, simply ignore it.

➤ If possible, always correct people in private so the individual can save face. If correction must be administered in public, be very deliberate with what you say and don't say. Public correction, administered poorly, can have catastrophic effects on the individual receiving the correction.

➤ Keep the correction focused on the behavior that needs correction, not the person.

➤ Use tactics like the sandwich method to cushion the blow.

CHAPTER 12
How to Be a Better Listener

Conversation in the United States is a competitive exercise in which the first person to draw breath is declared the listener.
—*Nathan Miller*

America is a nation of poor listeners. Whether you choose not to listen, or if you never learned how to properly listen in the first place, it impedes the flow of information between you and the people you are attempting to communicate with. In this chapter are listening techniques you can use to demonstrate that you're paying attention to what others are saying. When people feel like they are heard and understood, they feel more connected and less frustrated. You'll be able to use all these techniques today!

The only job of a listener is to be physically and mentally present when someone is talking, even if we are on the phone or connected to a meeting over the Internet. And just like there are tactics we can employ to be more effective speakers, there are also proven strategies we can use when listening. We are not born good listeners; most need to learn this important skill. Many of us learned poor listening behaviors from poor listeners, and that's all we know—no one ever showed us a better way.

Becoming a better listener is one of the foundational components of being a better communicator in general. In addition, the higher you go in any organization, the more becomes expected of you with regard to your ability to effectively listen. If you are in a leadership position, and you refuse to listen adequately, buckle up for a bumpy ride as this is guaranteed to cause problems among your peers and subordinates. Engineers take great exception to not being listened to because they feel like they were hired to steer the company from a technical standpoint. Failing to listen to them is equivalent to telling them that their years of experience and expertise aren't important. That's not the message you want to send.

From a business perspective, failure to listen properly impacts the bottom line. The authors of *Project Management for the Unofficial Project Manager* (Kory Kogon, Suzette Blakemore, and James Wood) summed it up perfectly by saying, "Failure to listen can lead to strained relationships, decreased productivity, missed learning opportunities, and damaging errors in judgment." It's easy to forget, but listening is at least as important as speaking. If we put great effort into choosing our words wisely, we should put the same amount of effort into listening effectively.

ARE YOU REALLY LISTENING?

When people talk to you, do you really listen to them? Do you actively participate in the conversation? Or, are you waiting for your turn to speak? Think about that for a minute. When someone is talking, are you

   a. Thinking about a point you wanted to make a while ago?
   b. Trying to figure out when you can squeeze in what you want to say?
   c. Not listening at all because you're thinking about something completely different but nodding like you're paying attention?

Personally, I've spent a lot of time in group (c).

It's common among engineers to listen only when something supports their predetermined position. This isn't listening, this is looking for agreement. It can be tempting to only want to consider ideas when they are in agreement with our own, but typically what happens is we don't fully consider what is being said by others because we are more interested in winning a disagreement than collaborating.

People seem to know when they've been heard and understood. You innately sense when others have been actively listening to you, internalized what you've said, and given you the appropriate verbal and nonverbal signals that indicate they've heard and understood you. You may have talked to a person and walked away saying to yourself, "She didn't hear a word I said." Oh, she heard all right; she just didn't listen. This kind of hearing creates problems in organizations. If you do this long enough, people become frustrated and find ways to work around you.

Listening to others is a key component to increasing our influence with them. If you want the best from the people around you, you'll need to listen more effectively.

LISTEN WITH YOUR BODY

The first listening technique has to do with the messages you send to another person nonverbally. The physical signals you give to others demonstrate you're actively listening to them. If you don't display them, people notice their absence and leave the conversation feeling like you might not have understood what they were trying to communicate.

In the 1960s, Dr. Albert Mehrabian of UCLA conducted a study to determine how much our communication of feelings and attitudes are based on nonverbals (tone of voice, facial expressions, etc.). He determined that 93 percent of those communications are nonverbal and only 7 percent are verbal. There are some disagreements regarding how applicable these numbers are to *all* of our communications, but when we consider how often our feelings and attitudes are a part of our daily conversations, it's easy to see how important nonverbal signals are to successfully communicate with another person. If you were to say the words "I'm fine" through clenched teeth while glaring at the person who asked you, what would come across to the listener is that you actually were *not* fine. This same concept is true with regards to listening.

Picture this: You're talking to your manager, and she is saying things like, "Yes, uh-huh, keep going," but she is looking all over the place the entire time trying to find someone. Is she really listening to you? No. Her actions are not in alignment with her words. To be effective communicators, we don't want to send mixed messages to the people we are listening to. *Demonstrate* to them that you are listening. Now, let's talk about some specific ways we can do that.

When people talk to you, face them. This physically demonstrates they have your attention. Squarely face the other person with your feet and shoulders. If you point your feet away from the person, this conveys that you want to leave because your feet typically point in the direction you want to go. If you face people square on, you are actively engaging them with your body. You're saying, "I am here, and I am listening to you." Another form of this would be to turn your body and chair toward someone who has come into your office or cubicle. If you keep your body pointed toward your monitor, and your hands on the keyboard, the message you're sending is: "I'm in the middle of something important. Hurry up and get this over with."

We see this concept of facing individuals play out when groups of people talk to each other. Individuals who are talking to each other naturally form a circle with all the people in it. If you are part of the circle, you're part of the conversation. If you're outside of the circle, you're not part of the conversation. Squarely facing a person with your feet and shoulders is creating a small, two-person communication circle.

Customs vary in different parts of the world, but for Western cultures, looking people in the eyes when you are talking with them is one of the most important nonverbal signals you can give to a speaker. Doing this sends the message that you are actively engaged, and they have your undivided attention. Looking all over the place or doing something else while they are talking to you communicates to the speaker that the current subject isn't important to you.

Crossing your arms is another physical signal that's easy to address. In short, don't do it. It's perceived as being standoffish and protective. In the book *What Every Body is Saying,* ex-FBI agent Joe Navarro says that leaving your arms relaxed at your sides is an effective way of communicating to speakers that you are no threat to them and helps put them at ease. This is especially important when approaching someone for the first time. You want to do everything in your power to make the person feel comfortable.

If you are talking with someone while you're sitting, sit up straight and lean forward a little with both feet on the ground. Leaning forward shows the person you're physically anticipating what is going to be said and you're interested. Act like the person is going to give you the winning lottery numbers. Your posture would be that of anticipation and excitement. If you have a notepad or laptop with you, it may be appropriate to put it in front of you and have your writing instrument available to take notes, if necessary. People really like it when you take notes when they speak. It physically communicates that what they are saying is so important you want to capture it for later use.

Don't slouch in your chair like the stereotypical, rebellious teenager. This sends a loud and clear statement that you think the discussion is boring and you want to leave. Many full-grown adults do this on a regular basis. It's easy to fix, so there is no reason not to. No one likes talking to an audience full of people who are communicating to you through nonverbal signals that they don't want to be there.

If your nonverbal signals are in conflict with your words, people will always go with your nonverbals because they are more reliable. Don't send I'm-not-listening signals with your body. *Always be aware of the signals your actions are sending because listeners rely a great deal on them to determine if their communication was successful.*

DON'T INTERRUPT

Interrupting someone while they are speaking is equivalent to telling them to shut up—right now! It's a terrible habit that often goes unnoticed by people who do it the most because it's become a core part of how they communicate. It's become a bad habit.

Interrupting people while they are talking is flat-out rude. How are people supposed to interpret being continually cut off before they can finish? When you cut people off, what you are effectively saying is that their current train of thought is so unimportant to you that you've decided to stop them in their tracks and say something of your own. It's akin to saying, "Yeah, yeah, whatever you're saying is fine, but let me tell you something more important."

Interrupting people creates an arms race. People know that if they want to finish a thought, they either have to talk faster or interrupt you in return. Perhaps you really needed to hear what the person was going to say, but now you won't because you couldn't wait the extra minute to let them finish.

Instead of interrupting, be patient. To be blunt, it's basic good manners. You may feel like you must interject something into a conversation at that very moment, but you really don't. If you have scratch paper or a notebook handy, write down your points. You can come back to those when that person is done, and you can share your thoughts then. Let the person who is talking finish. You'll get your chance to speak.

Some engineers have expressed concern that when talking with certain individuals, they may never get a chance to speak if they don't interrupt. You may know these types of people, too. It's very rare, however, that you *never* get a chance to talk. You just may have to wait longer to do it. In the end, if someone completely dominates a conversation, and you have important information to share, you may have to continue the conversation later or use a different communication channel.

If you're constantly on the receiving end of being cut off, I feel for you. I really do. With certain engineers, it seems like I'm being interrupted on every single statement. It's *very* frustrating. Instead of effectively communicating, I want to run out the front door screaming so I can let out all the built-up frustration. To deal with it maturely, I accept the fact that the person communicates that way right now. I accept that I'll probably be interrupted continually during our conversation, so I prepare for it. Sometimes that little mental adjustment is enough to get me through it.

Take note of how long *you* talk when you're engaged in conversations. Do you give people enough space to contribute to the topic being discussed? Do people feel like they have to interrupt you because you talk too much? If you think you're talking too much, you probably are.

DEMONSTRATE YOU UNDERSTAND

To demonstrate to a speaker that you understand what they're saying, paraphrase what has been said at different points in the conversation. This serves two purposes:

1. It allows you to prove that you've been paying attention.
2. If you misunderstood, it gives the other person a chance to correct you.

It's similar to using the steering wheel to keep your car on a straight road. These tiny corrections keep you from ending up in a ditch. If you periodically paraphrase what has been said, it keeps you from getting too far away from the intent of the speaker by correcting your understanding, or at least checking to make sure you're still on course.

As an example, say you're a graphic designer and your employer approaches you about the work you've done on a recent project. He is concerned because the project you just finished isn't what he had in mind for an upcoming company-wide promotion. He doesn't believe it's in line with the company's branding identity. After he finishes, you paraphrase what he said by saying: "So, you don't think this reflects our company's brand because of the choice of colors I used. You'd also like me to put more emphasis on a specific aspect of the promotion and show you the changes on Thursday." Your employer can either agree with you or correct your understanding by restating what he is trying to communicate.

See how this works? You're testing the speaker to make sure both of you are talking about the same thing. Sometimes what someone is trying to say and how they are saying it are off, and paraphrasing what you think they said can do wonders for making sure their intent is coming across correctly. I've seen two people that had just sat in the *exact* same meeting walk away with a completely different interpretation of what was said. No one double-checked their understanding.

I first learned about this technique in Robert Bolton's book *People Skills: How to Assert Yourself, Listen to Others, and Resolve Conflicts*. I was a little apprehensive concerning its effectiveness. To me, it seemed odd to blurt out a statement basically telling someone what they had already said in a much-condensed form. I was wrong. The people I've talked with haven't thought anything of it. In fact, they seemed to appreciate the feedback. Give it a try for yourself. Like anything else, it may take a little bit of practice to figure out the appropriate places to paraphrase, but when you do, you'll show the people you are talking with that you understand the information they are trying to convey.

DON'T HIJACK THE CONVERSATION

When someone hijacks an airplane, what happens? A person on board a plane forcibly takes control of the aircraft and announces to everyone that they are now going to a different destination. The same thing happens when engineers are engaged in conversation. One engineer will be talking about a certain subject, and another engineer will change the topic to talk about what they want instead. This is called hijacking the conversation. It's another poor listening habit we are going to try to break.

Hijacking conversations is so prevalent most people don't recognize when it's happening anymore—we've been conditioned to accept it. As a result, our conversations become a mess because neither party stays on a subject long enough to let the other person finish their train of thought. The whole point of the interaction is missed because both parties focus on talking and neither is listening. Their conversation bounces all over the place.

Engineers really struggle in this area because of their analytical nature. During conversations and especially meetings, if anything incorrect is said, there can be a tendency for them to want to correct the error, thus creating a "fork" in the discussion that can hijack the main topic and cause everyone to start talking about the new issue. This change in the conversation is often called a rabbit hole, but some also call it a rabbit trail. Taking these conversational side quests can waste a lot of time and energy because there is a potential that we never make it back to the topic we were discussing originally—the reason we decided to have a meeting in the first place.

Let people finish what they are saying. You'll get your chance to comment. After one subject is finished, a new one naturally will evolve. Give others the time they need to finish sharing what's on their minds. People really appreciate this because they feel they've been heard.

Conversation is fluid, and you can't put hard and fast limits on what takes place during one. You can, however, fix a lot of common problems by walking into a conversation with the intent of listening more and not violating the handful of principles presented here. One of the primary ways you learn is by listening. If you want to have more of a positive impact on the people around you, become an actively engaged listener.

SUMMARY

- Listening is just as important as speaking.

- Are you really listening or just waiting for a chance to talk?

- Be conscious of nonverbals when listening. Speakers will always go with the messages our body is broadcasting if they are in conflict with what we are saying—nonverbals are more reliable.

- Interrupting someone when they are speaking is rude and can be a bad habit. It's like telling someone to shut up.

- Give the right nonverbal signals during conversations. Paraphrase what was said to prove you understand.

- Don't hijack conversations. Let people finish their train of thought before switching topics on them.

CHAPTER 13

Design and Code Reviews

Jimmy Developer joined your team a couple months ago right out of college and is excited about committing code for his first major deliverable. With stars in his eyes, Jimmy believes anything is possible. He *knows* that the solutions to poverty and hunger are only a few well-thought-out lines of code away. His current deliverable is his big opportunity to impress those around him and prove he's going to be a truly great engineer. The only problem is his code is bad. Really bad. What do you do as one of his code reviewers? Do you crush his dreams and give him a dose of reality as you see it? Or, do you water this little green sprout peeking through the soil and encourage, develop, and guide him using your years of experience and knowledge? The choice is yours.

If you are a software engineer, and you hear the phrase "code review," what immediately comes to mind? Do you start breathing fast and begin playing the music to the movie *Jaws* in your head (da-duh, da-duh)? If so, you've probably been on the receiving end of some brutal code reviews. Depending on who's reviewing your code and how they do it, you can walk away feeling mentored and enlightened, or leave feeling like you just went ten rounds with a professional heavyweight fighter.

When you review code, you can apply people-skills principles to increase the chances that the necessary changes are made *and* the individual whose work you are reviewing interprets the correction in a positive, helpful way. Code reviews can and should be one of the primary ways to help people sharpen their technical skills. Viewed in that light, take extra care to make sure you don't blow a good opportunity to mentor and guide a fellow engineer.

Before getting started, answer this question: What is the purpose of a code or design review? If your answer is about ensuring adherence to the original design, maintaining (or increasing) product quality, and teaching, you're right on target. Code reviews have nothing to do with settling a score, berating others, or showing your technical superiority. When done correctly, code reviews are one of the most powerful training opportunities available to your team. When more engineers are doing the right things on future deliverables, your team benefits.

This chapter focuses specifically on code reviews, but with very little effort, the core principles could be applied to most any type of review conducted in any engineering field. Many of the underlying problems encountered when reviewing another's work have nothing to do with the specific type of work being reviewed. Instead, they have to do with human behavior, and the correct way of pointing out mistakes while keeping a co-worker motivated and excited to do a better job the next time around.

FACE-TO-FACE REVIEWS ARE BEST

Tools can be used to facilitate code reviews, but they are not a replacement for face-to-face interactions. Review tools do a great job of showing *what* has changed, but they don't necessarily capture *why* it was changed. In order to get the full picture of why something was implemented a specific way, you need to be able to ask questions.

Many tasks are easier when you have a back-and-forth discussion in real time with another person, and code reviews are one of those tasks. You *can* conduct moderate-to-complex code reviews completely through a review tool, but walking a few aisles down and engaging in a focused discussion about the changes can be far more productive.

If face-to-face interaction is not possible, hold a video conference or call the individual who submitted the changes. The live interaction allows questions to go both ways so that decisions are clarified with the least amount of overhead possible. This is more time efficient than having to write short, cryptic notes using your code review tool. A video conference or phone call also pushes the review to completion in a timely fashion. Emails sent via a review tool are easy to ignore and often get buried under the mountain of logging alert emails, meeting invites, and security awareness training messages.

I once heard a story about two engineers conducting a heated debate using a code review tool as the backdrop. One engineer put a page worth of antagonistic comments in the tool about a change to the code base. In reply, the other engineer put in a page of his own. There was likely more at play here than a simple code review, but you get the point: A lot of back-and-forth writing is eliminated if you can sit down and hammer out the details of a change and personal differences, if needed.

CODE: IT IS PERSONAL

As a software engineer, I know coding can be a very personal thing. In a way, it's like putting your thoughts down "on paper" for everyone else to see. Depending on the difficulty of the problem you're trying to solve, it may take weeks to come up with a solution before you even start writing your first line of code. When you're done, your ideas and past experiences are put into a computer via a programming language to solve a problem. The resulting solution can be very personal. To some software engineers, code is viewed as an extension of themselves, so a code review feels more like a personal attack than a professional analysis of the work under review.

A software engineer may be extremely self-conscious about the code they've written and dread code reviews. Senior Software Engineer Aaron Krogh said: "Developers have this weird attachment to their code. This causes conflict when someone tweaks their stuff." This phenomenon is not isolated to just writing software. Anyone having their work reviewed, critiqued, or changed can feel anxious and defensive when others pick it apart. Engineers are no different when it comes to being evaluated and scrutinized. Having an analytical personality doesn't mean you're devoid of all feelings and emotions.

When you're asked to review someone else's work, it can be helpful to communicate your purpose up front, and let them know you are there to help. Sure, you're required to verify the changes are implemented to specification and to make sure there are no unanticipated side effects from the changes, but you can also use your reviews as a mentoring opportunity. Done correctly and tactfully, the review can teach a fellow engineer how to correct what was specifically done wrong *and* give you the opportunity to impart more technical wisdom in related areas. Reviews can be much more valuable when they are done in a way that doesn't foster an atmosphere of fear and dread. If engineers in your organization dread code reviews, you're doing something wrong. If you have to be a jerk to make sure quality work is produced, something is wrong with either you or the people on your team. Quality, self-motivated engineers don't need fear and public shaming to do what's right. They do what's right because of who they are.

DON'T BE OVERLY CRITICAL

If you're overly critical of someone's code, it's hard for that person to *not* take it personally. Some engineers will take your criticism as a direct blow to their intelligence, which was *not* likely your intent when reviewing their work. Being aware of this beforehand allows you to approach the review more strategically. Remember, you live or die as a team. You want your team members to push the boundaries and share their best and most creative ideas. If you're overly critical of the work your team members are doing, you'll never see their best stuff because they'll only share what's least likely to be criticized. Mark my words: Criticism shuts down creativity!

You might be an extremely gifted engineer, but not everyone may be at your level yet. Teams and companies have people at varying degrees of ability. Just like how professional sports teams have stars, engineering teams also have stars that possess more natural ability than others. If you are one of those people with advanced engineering powers, use your enhanced ability to raise up those around you instead of lording it over them. You might get a quick high from putting someone in their place with your exceptional abilities, but you've also sown a bad seed with that person that *will* affect future interactions. Do you want people to actively limit their exposure to you because you ignore basic people skills? Nobody *has to* work with a difficult engineer. If we make it bad enough for others, they'll simply leave and go somewhere else.

While conducting your code reviews, avoid being overly critical by separating your opinion about coding style from the purpose of the review, such as ensuring the bug or feature in question was properly fixed or implemented. If someone used a for-loop instead of a lambda expression, does it really matter? If there are no clear-cut guidelines for the way a problem should be solved, consider throwing out your preference and leave it up to them. That may sound like technical heresy, but some things don't really matter all that much. It's more important for the engineer submitting the work to feel empowered to solve technical problems in a way that makes sense to them. If your project is extremely sensitive to performance, or you have strict coding guidelines for some parts of your system, enforce them. If not, consider letting personal taste regarding the formatting of inline code comments slide.

If you are one of those engineers that are very opinionated about coding style, consider putting a "best practices" guide together for the languages you use. This might be a great opportunity for you to connect with other engineers and also allow you to publish your style preferences for everyone else to use. This way everyone can get what they want: The style sticklers can have an external reference to point to when code isn't up to the standard, and committers can have a resource they can use *beforehand* to speed up code reviews (and limit critical feedback). Static analysis tools can help in this area, too, because they remove any person-to-person conflict.

WAYS TO APPROACH CORRECTION

It's unavoidable. At some point, you'll have to correct the work of other engineers. If you're a senior engineer, reviewing and correcting others' work is a significant part of your daily routine. *How* you go about administering this correction makes all the difference in the world. Done properly, you create an atmosphere of openness, creativity, and learning. Done incorrectly, you create an environment where team members are afraid to share ideas because of the fear of public criticism. Which team would *you* rather be part of?

Asking questions to lead engineers to their own mistakes is one of the most simple and effective ways to administer correction. To remove any potential for person-to-person conflict from the interaction, ask questions like, "Why did you decide to do X instead of Y?" or "Have you seen this before?" as you show them an example of the right way to accomplish something. Correction administered using thoughtful questions is exponentially easier for engineers to take than pointing at their code, laughing, and saying it's the worst thing you've ever seen. You may think I'm making this up, but I once floated one of my ideas past another engineer, and he told me the idea was "the stupidest thing you could do." He meant it in a very derogatory way, too! I laughed at the time because his response was so over the top, but I couldn't believe he said that to me. Did it mortally wound me? No, but responses like that are unnecessary and counterproductive. Saying "I'm not sure that's going to work because of X" takes roughly the same amount of energy as saying, "You're an idiot!" Pick the one with the least number of negative side effects. Can you get people to do the right thing through fear and intimidation? Yes, but again, it creates unnecessary interpersonal strife at the same time.

In a previous chapter, the sandwich method was presented as a popular approach to administering correction. This tactic is very effective in the context of design and code reviews. For example, if someone has implemented logic with a bug in it, during the review you could say: "I like how you've broken up your code into easy-to-understand blocks. It's easy to follow. I noticed, however, that there appears to be a logic bug in routine X. No problem, that's why we do code reviews. This code is going to be really easy to maintain when you're done." See how easy that is to do? The correction about the logic bug is in the middle of two *true* positives (not lies or flattery). This method can be used all the time and not only in code reviews. Use it in emails and everyday person-to-person interactions. It's easy to do, accomplishes the original goal of correcting the work, and is significantly easier to take if you're the one being corrected.

When reviewing code (or anything for that matter), there can be a tendency to want to focus almost exclusively on its shortcomings. This tendency makes sense, since the primary focus of reviewing someone's work is to make sure there aren't major gaps and that the work actually addresses the problem it's trying to solve. The problem with this approach, however, is the review can quickly become lopsided. If all the feedback is negative, it can give the person being reviewed a skewed perception of what was done.

While reviewing an engineer's work, intentionally highlight what they did *right,* too. From a software engineering perspective, if they included a thorough set of unit and system tests, point that out, emphasizing how important it is to make sure the system stays healthy in the future. If they implemented a piece of logic in a particularly interesting way, such as being elegant or easy to follow, praise them for it. Praise and commendations go a long way in establishing a healthy rapport with engineers, and it encourages the good behaviors our fellow engineers are *already* demonstrating.

If you've read many personal-growth books, you've read about the concept of praising the behaviors you want to see more often. Whatever coding or design principles you want to see more of, call those out and praise them during your reviews. Because people, even engineers, crave appreciation and praise, they'll willingly start doing the right things more often because they want additional recognition.

When going through another engineer's work, if you once struggled with the very same thing they are currently having difficulty with, you'll want to make sure and point that out. Doing this can go a long way in diffusing any potential conflict because it communicates to the engineer whose work is currently being reviewed that no one is perfect—especially you.

If you're conducting a review as a group, and it becomes apparent that what's been submitted is totally unacceptable, avoid creating a feeding frenzy. Like sharks, engineers seem to smell blood in the water. After the group has established the work under review is egregiously wrong, call off the review and reschedule it rather than going through the entire review and enumerating in great detail everything that's wrong with the code. Complete the review in phases. Give the developer feedback on the most serious flaws in their work and let them fix those before meeting again for the next round of corrections. This will save everyone time *and* allow the author of the code to save face.

If you want to be more skillful in dealing with people, you may have to change some of your current behaviors. Don't be so quick to dismiss the softer aspects of dealing with people because they have a real, tangible impact on the bottom line effectiveness of your teams. You can improve your people skills without sacrificing the quality of your work or the standards within your team. Simply become more aware of the people aspect of your work and use all the tools at your disposal to draw out the best in the people you work with. You can set a high technical bar for your teams *and* do it in a way that encourages inclusiveness, growth, and creativity. You can have your cake and eat it, too.

SUMMARY

- Face-to-face reviews are best because they encourage real time, back-and-forth discussions. They are also faster and harder to ignore, unlike emails sent from review tools.

- Many engineers look at their work as an extension of themselves, like an artist or musician. Being overly critical of their work is akin to criticizing their abilities and intelligence.

- You may be an extremely talented engineer, but not everyone is. Use your enhanced ability to assist the other engineers around you. Criticizing others is easy. Making people better is much more challenging and worthwhile.

- Ask questions to lead people to their mistakes.

- Use the sandwich method when correcting others.

- Always praise the good aspects of the work being reviewed, even if you have to dig to find any.

CHAPTER 14

Running a Productive Meeting

Formal meetings are a part of corporate life and that's not going to change any time soon. Regardless of how much engineers dislike them, there are times when getting people together is the best and most productive way to solve an issue or disseminate information.

Because meetings are a social endeavor, they fall under the people-skills umbrella along with everything else in the previous chapters. If you show up to your meetings late, unprepared, and unfocused, people's opinions of you may turn negative quickly, especially if there are individuals in attendance you've never formally met before.

Meetings may be the only platform you have to demonstrate your skills and abilities to people outside your immediate team. For instance, if you give a presentation on a project you've completed, and the vice president of marketing decides to show up, this may be your best opportunity to make a good impression. You may not get another chance to show this individual what you can do and the quality of your work.

This chapter has tips on how to make your meetings more professional and productive and less likely to leave a bad impression on the people in attendance. By applying a handful of known best practices, you'll have greater success when facilitating your meetings.

DO YOU REALLY NEED A MEETING?

It can be tempting to think, "I'll just pull everyone together really quick to discuss this new issue that popped up"—but is that the right thing to do? Do you *really* need a meeting, or in reality do you only need input from a few key people? Can you just as easily get the answer you're looking for via email or a couple quick personal visits? If a meeting is not necessary, don't waste people's time.

Recurrent meetings should be treated the same way. If there are no planned topics, ask the expected attendees if they have anything pressing that needs to be covered and if not, cancel the meeting. Don't feel obligated to hold a meeting just because it's on the calendar. In fact, look for reasons to cancel planned meetings unless the agenda will add value to those who attend.

If you cancel a meeting, do it early enough so people know they have an open slot on their calendar for other work. If you cancel right before the scheduled time slot, the attendees miss an opportunity to utilize that extra time most effectively. Typically, no one has a problem with last-minute meeting cancellations, but these types of cancellations can cause disruptions to work plans for those of us who like to optimize our daily schedule ahead of time.

If you're not familiar with the story of *The Boy Who Cried Wolf*, here it is in a nutshell. A young boy, who watched a flock of sheep near a village, repeatedly brought villagers to his aid by falsely crying out, "Wolf! Wolf!" When his neighbors came to help him, he laughed at them for believing his false alarms. Eventually, a real wolf came, and no one responded to his cries for help because they had been conditioned to ignore him.

Calling meetings when they aren't necessary is akin to crying wolf. Schedule meetings only when there's a real issue, or wolf, that needs to be addressed by the group. If you continually schedule unneeded meetings, engineers will find ways to skip out or bring their laptops and do something else while the meeting is going on. They may be physically present, but their minds will be someplace else.

BEFORE THE MEETING

For anything but quick focus-room (dedicated impromptu meeting spaces many companies have) meetings, there is a certain amount of preparation you should do to make sure your meetings are conducted in a professional manner and achieve the stated purpose. Failing to properly prepare for meetings can decrease meeting productivity and syphon away time that could have been used for more important tasks. In this section, we'll cover the basic preparation tasks you should do well before the day of the meeting.

First, determine how long the meeting should be. Meetings typically use most of the time scheduled for them, even if it's not necessary. If you want a short meeting, reserve less time for it. Long meetings are generally a bad idea for technical discussions. Details start slipping through the cracks as attention spans wane.

As the meeting facilitator, you must develop a clear agenda. Thinking ahead of time about the topics you want to cover helps you decide if you need a meeting in the first place. Sometimes a meeting is a knee-jerk reaction to a problem that can, and should, be solved via a different communication avenue. If you don't have an agenda, you probably should wait to schedule the meeting. When you do send out the meeting invite, attach the agenda so your invitees can look it over and properly prepare. A clear agenda will also help optional invitees decide if they should attend.

Determine who needs to attend the meeting based on how much the topic impacts their projects. In tools like Microsoft Outlook, you can mark invitees as required or optional as part of the official invitation that's sent out. This is a key indicator to the recipient as to whether they really need to attend or whether you are inviting them because you *think* they might have some interest in what's being discussed. Don't abuse this. Give invitees the choice of how to spend their time if they aren't truly required to be at the meeting.

If you'll be reviewing technical material at your meeting, provide enough time for people to review it beforehand. Send out the appropriate documents or weblinks early enough so the other engineers have time to look them over and prepare thoughtful input. If you don't do this, you may not get the feedback you need. Some people won't review the material no matter how long you give them. Don't get offended by this. Instead, be respectful of the engineers who *will* look it over by sending it out well in advance of the meeting.

Prior to the day of the meeting, make sure you know how to use the audio and video equipment. Come in on a different day to allow yourself time to tinker with it, if need be. Your attendees may become unhappy and impatient if ten minutes of a thirty-minute meeting are wasted while you try to figure out how to get the projector working or the virtual meeting started. It's a waste of everybody's time and may cause the meeting to run long because you weren't able to start on time.

If you don't have anything scheduled before your meeting, show up a little early and get everything set up and working properly before everyone else arrives. Confirm that nothing has changed since your initial check the day before. Being early also gives you a few minutes to meet and converse with others who arrive early. It's a good time to get to know them a little better.

If it's an early morning meeting, consider providing donuts or coffee. Buying donuts for an early meeting is an engineer's way of thanking the attendees for coming. If the meeting is over lunch, will the company provide food? If not, maybe you want to buy lunch out of your own pocket as a way of appreciating your attendees. If lunch cannot be provided, let your attendees know to bring their lunches to the meeting. Doing things like this show people that their time is valuable and that you know you have inconvenienced them in some small way.

DURING THE MEETING

You have an 11:00 a.m. meeting down the hall in the big conference room. To be a good corporate citizen, you leave your workspace five minutes early to make sure you're not late because you're keenly aware of how your punctuality is interpreted by others. You usually show up a few minutes early because you want to be settled *before* the meeting starts, and you especially don't want people to be waiting on you. When 11:00 a.m. rolls around, the person who scheduled the meeting isn't present. At 11:05 a.m., still not there. Finally, almost ten minutes past the hour, the meeting organizer shows up *to his own meeting.*

From a people-skills perspective, showing up late to meetings is a poor reflection on your character, and implies the meeting isn't important to you. If it was important, you would have been on time. If the meeting organizer was handing out duffle bags stuffed with one-hundred-dollar bills, you'd have been on time. Don't be the person that others make fun of because they're chronically late for meetings.

I've had people schedule meetings with me, and then completely blow me off, and not even for any good reason—they were simply having a casual conversation with someone else and didn't want to stop. I don't hold it against them, but the message they are sending is loud and clear: Their current conversation about what food their cat likes is more important than the meeting they scheduled with me. If you are scheduled to attend a meeting with someone, you have two acceptable courses of action:

1. Cancel ahead in a reasonable amount of time.
2. Follow through with your commitment.

Anything else sends the wrong message.

Punctuality to meetings is important, and there are things you can do to ensure you stay on track throughout your day. For example, you can leave your previous meetings a little early, so you're on time to your next scheduled appointment. Make it clear to everyone that you have to leave early because it's important to get to your next meeting on time. No one will tell you no and they probably wish more people operated like that when attending *their* meetings.

When planning your meeting, if certain attendees are only needed for part of it, consider cutting them loose when they are done contributing. If an engineer will only contribute a small portion to the meeting, put them first on the agenda so they can leave when their part is done. In practice, this method works quite well, and the individual appreciates being allowed to leave early and get back to their work.

During your meeting, you're responsible for taking notes unless you appoint someone else to that role. Take your laptop or a notebook and record what is being discussed during the meeting. If you have your laptop, one approach you can use is to compose a new email in real time with the notes of the meeting. That way you can capture what is being discussed and immediately send out the information as soon as the meeting is over. You won't have to transcribe the notes to a different medium, either, because they are already in a shareable form. Alternatively, you can also add to or create new pages within your internal documentation tools, such as SharePoint or Confluence, while the meeting is in progress. As soon as the meeting is over, the content is available to everyone.

When you facilitate a meeting, keep the meeting on track and progressing along your predetermined agenda. You can't allow your meeting to be hijacked and steered in a completely different direction. If an issue comes up that might derail the meeting, let the attendees know you've captured the topic in your notes and will address it later. Rarely does someone bring up a new topic that is significant enough to completely subvert the current meeting in progress. Most distractions are caused by engineers getting overly hung up on technical details that can be discussed at a later time.

If you're done discussing what was planned, don't be afraid to end early. You're not obligated to use the entire time, and you don't have to drag unrelated topics out of people. Some engineers can't stand silence and will start talking about random things to fill the void. This is a waste of time. Before you close the meeting, ask if there is anything else that needs to be discussed, give about two or three seconds for a response, and then cut everyone loose if no one speaks up. If you wait any longer than that, someone will crack under the pressure to break the silence and begin talking.

As the meeting organizer and facilitator, it's your responsibility to end on time, which is just as important as starting on time. Scheduling a thirty-minute meeting and going twenty minutes over is unacceptable. You either did a poor job of keeping the meeting on track, or you grossly underestimated the time required to cover the subject. Don't make everyone else pay for your mistake unless everyone agrees to it.

If your meeting is approaching the scheduled end time and the group won't be able to cover the topic as expected, a good tactic is to ask everyone what they would like to do. Do they want to stay late and finish up, or would they rather schedule a follow-up meeting? If everyone is engaged in the topic and has the extra time, finishing up may be the most effective thing to do. However, if people have other activities scheduled, and they usually do, you don't want to make them late for their next commitment. Keeping only half the group together means key people would miss important information. If this situation arises, schedule a follow-up meeting while everyone is together. You want everyone present for the rest of the discussion.

AFTER THE MEETING

After the meeting, send a follow-up email containing the notes that were captured and any important supplemental links. The attendees will have access to the information and weblinks referred to without having to contact you for the information. Additionally, thank anyone who attended and contributed in a way you considered above and beyond what was expected. This is a good opportunity to make a deposit in their interpersonal bank accounts.

SUMMARY

➤ Do you really need a meeting? If not, don't schedule one.

➤ Carefully consider how long the meeting should be, and who should be required to attend versus who might be interested in attending.

➤ Know how to use the equipment in the room. Go to the room the day before the meeting if you are unfamiliar with how to operate the equipment.

➤ Be on time to your own meeting.

➤ Cut people loose after they have contributed their part. Start the meeting with those individuals, if possible.

➤ It is your responsibility to take notes, keep the meeting on track, and end on time.

CHAPTER 15

Talking to Non-Technical People

Have you ever gone to the doctor, mechanic, or lawyer and had a hard time understanding exactly what was being said because they used too much domain-specific jargon? ("You're going to stick the what, where?") If so, you're not alone.

Unfortunately, using domain-specific jargon is a common practice in engineering circles, too. Engineers are so mired in the details all day long they forget others don't have the same context and vocabulary as they do. They will happily explain a complicated feature or technical aspect of a product to someone without realizing they're doing very little communicating—their audience is struggling to decode the message. Many times, the listener will nod like they understand so they don't look unintelligent, but in reality, they understood only a small fraction of what was said. They then go back to their teams and try to convey what they *think* they heard. This is a recipe for disaster.

I like to joke with people by telling them my wife hasn't really known what I've done as a profession since we first exchanged wedding vows over two decades ago. When we were first married, I was a Patriot Missile Mechanic and Operator in the United States Army, stationed at Ft. Bliss, Texas. She could understand statements like, "I sit in a small van, and protect important things from enemy planes and missiles." Past that, she was lost. If I threw in all the domain-specific acronyms (good grief, the army has a lot of acronyms), her eyes would glaze over and she'd stop listening out of self-preservation. If I wanted her to understand something, I had to keep it simple, not because she's dumb, but because it was a foreign language to her.

After I was discharged from the army, I attended college where I earned a bachelor of science in computer science. Now, instead of saying, "I sit in a small van," I say, "I write software that helps customers use my company's products and solutions." If I told her I was working on integrating our billing framework with a third-party eCommerce solution using a SaaS-based message-queuing solution to bridge Virtual Private Clouds in Amazon Web Services, she'd be totally confused because she doesn't have the necessary background to understand anything I just said.

The same thing can happen with people you work with. They may not have the same technical background as you, and all you may do is confuse them with the technical details. The whole point of communication is to transfer information. If you're speaking like you're from another dimension, and use a lot of engineering terminology, very little information transfer may be taking place.

Using too many technical details doesn't impress people; it frustrates them. People from your company's marketing, sales, and other non-technical departments don't care about the details you spend all day obsessing over. It's your job to worry about them, not theirs. They only want to know enough to move forward with *their* deliverables. As Senior Software Engineer Aaron Krogh put it; "I can't tell you how many times in a big meeting I've seen some single developer go on a rant about the memory structure of Python variables, or garbage collection heaps in .NET. Your boss doesn't care, let alone understand.

Convey pertinent information, not the information *you* would want to hear but what you need to say to converse properly."

Refusing to adjust your message to your audience is an extremely lazy form of communication. What we do is hard, and trying to explain it to someone without the necessary background can be difficult. So, what do we do? Do we give up and blast our intended audience with acronyms, low-level details, and hipster technology names because it's easier for us? Or, do we realize that our audience needs the information we have, and unless we meet their needs, they may end up making uninformed and misguided decisions based on what they *think* they understood? Trust me, it's worth the time to consciously think about what level of detail we need to communicate to our audience and dial it in appropriately. If we need to talk to someone like we are speaking to our grandmother, then so be it. We don't do it in a condescending way, but with tact and thoughtfulness so we can meet the needs of our listeners.

Communicating highly technical details in a way a non-engineer can understand them can be a very sought-after skill. It is not easy to take complex information and distill it into a form that someone with very little domain expertise can understand. It's a very promotable skill to be able to communicate effectively across your organization, regardless of the audience. You become a translator of sorts for people who need to know the "nuts and bolts" of the information without all the confusing details that can sometimes accompany it. If we, as engineers, can develop this ability to effectively communicate with others, regardless of their role in our organization, we can check off another box on the list of sought-after traits when it comes time to promote someone to a position of greater influence within our teams.

The higher the person is in your organization, the less detail they need. As Dave Hendricksen, the author of *The 12 Essential Skills for Software Architects,* wrote, "As a general rule of thumb, the amount of detailed information needed is inversely proportional to the person's level in the organization." There is a reason why an executive summary contains information specifically tailored for someone higher up in your organization. This also implies that all summaries are not the same and need to be adjusted based on your audience. Gauge your audience and tune your message appropriately. Know when to stop with the technical stuff.

Not every manager has a deep technical background. Some managers were engineers for only a very short time before realizing they wanted to move into management. Because of this, they never developed the background to engage in deep technical discussions. Some managers have *no technical background at all*. In order to help them manage our teams effectively, sometimes we have to figure out where they are technically, and then meet them there. Confusing the person who is in charge of managing your team's time and resources will only make their jobs harder, which in turn makes *your* job harder. The sooner you can figure out what level of detail your manager can handle, the sooner you can start communicating effectively.

The next meeting or one-on-one appointment you're in, think about where the other individual fits into your organization. If they are not part of your department or section, tailor what you say to their perceived level of understanding. If you worked in marketing, what would you want to hear from an engineer? If you were a C-class manager abstracted from the day-to-day details of feature development, what would you need to hear to make more informed decisions? They'll appreciate it because they don't have to unwind all the technical information, and you'll be more satisfied because you'll have done your part in making sure upper management is operating on current, accurate, and *understandable* information about your business.

SUMMARY

➤ Domain-specific technical jargon will confuse and frustrate your audience if they don't have the necessary engineering background.

➤ If you aren't transferring information, you aren't communicating and that can cause organizational problems.

➤ Tune your content based on your audience. Gauge where they are at and speak in terms they can understand.

CHAPTER 16

Mentorship

I've read and listened to a considerable amount of personal-growth material over the past few years. One topic that keeps coming up over and over is mentorship: The process of meeting with and learning from people more experienced than you. Without a doubt, mentorship is a very effective personal growth strategy because you learn from individuals who already have been where you want to go. There's power in knowing where some of the land mines are along the journey. What's not so obvious are the significant benefits of being a mentor for *someone else* and raising *them* up to a higher level.

Having mentored people for years, I cannot overstate how truly invigorating mentoring can be. Yes, it's work at times, but it's for a purpose. You're investing in the career of another person. What other activities have such a profound and personal impact on someone? Figuratively speaking, it's like reaching down, grabbing a person's hand, and pulling them up to where you are. It's one of the most rewarding things I do in life. Mentoring someone with the correct motives gives you a broader sense of purpose and gives you something you can point to and say, "See, this world is better for me being here."

Most of us, on our current path through life, will quickly be forgotten when we pass away—we have very little positive influence on those around us. The only thing that will carry on after we're gone is the time and energy invested in others. If you want to make a difference, at some point, your life needs to become more about other people; because by yourself, you really can't get much done. Big goals, like family, business, and community goals, need lots of people. Without leaders and influencers, many people will end up wandering around aimlessly like ants without a trail to follow. You can help them find their trail.

As a rule, people are almost completely self-focused and totally consumed with their own personal wellbeing. Mentorship provides an opportunity to put some of your focus on others. You can share your wisdom and experience with someone who needs encouragement. As a personal testimony, I can say that as soon as I stopped constantly obsessing over what I wanted and what wasn't working in my life, I immediately became happier. Being a mentor brings perspective to your life.

As an engineer, you've been gifted with above-average intelligence. This intelligence gives you an enhanced ability to understand complicated information and solve difficult problems. Spending this ability solely on personal gain is setting the bar low on what you can accomplish in life. Mentoring another engineer gives you the connection you need to transfer your knowledge, experience, and insights to another person. In a way, it's sort of like cloning a part of yourself.

WHY MENTORING IS GOOD FOR YOUR COMPANY

Engineers leave companies because they feel disconnected from their co-workers. Mentorship helps address this issue by creating stronger connections between individuals. As Simon Sinek, author of *Start With Why: How Great Leaders Inspire Everyone to Take Action* put it: "When we feel like we belong, we feel connected and we feel safe. As humans we crave the feeling and we seek it out." Being on the outside of something means you are one step closer to leaving. It's easy to leave something you never felt a part of in the first place.

When joining a team, an engineer is going to have a lot of questions. Joining a new team can be hard. Without a mentor, they may feel like they are constantly bugging their co-workers for help. In front of them is a figurative mountain of processes, tools, technologies, existing work, and social integration that must be climbed. A mentor can be a lifeline for an employee because the new team member now has a resource available to them who has volunteered to climb the mountain with them.

Your company wants people on the inside, connected and contributing all their talents and abilities. A formal mentorship program *shows* employees that their growth is important to the overall health of the business because top-notch engineering talent is being directed toward helping them grow. Not every lesson should be learned through your own personal failures. It's easier to learn from someone else's failures and save yourself the time and frustration.

Mentors aid in short-circuiting common technical and social mistakes that new employees may not be aware they are making. Mentorship is also a quick and easy way to bring new employees or team members up to speed on how work gets done in your organization—it's an effective way to show them the ropes.

IF YOU DON'T HAVE A MENTOR, GET ONE

Everyone reading this book has room to grow. Regardless of age or engineering hours logged, you have areas of your life that can be improved. A senior engineer may need career mentorship just as much or more than a new hire does. Thinking you've arrived can be one of the biggest hindrances to personal growth because you've convinced yourself you don't need to do any more growing.

You don't have to limit your personal growth to only engineering knowledge. For instance, many other areas may have just as much impact on your career progression and overall happiness as technical knowledge does. Learning how to become a better leader can positively impact other areas of our lives in a *significant* way. *Everyone* can learn from a mentor, and it doesn't have to be a mentor in a field directly related to our engineering profession.

Have you ever heard the old saying, "You have not because you ask not"? This maxim is especially true when it comes to finding a good quality mentor. Many times, you don't get the best mentors available simply because you don't ask. You may think the prospective mentors are too busy or too important to spend time with you. That was my attitude until I started applying a "What's the worse they are going to say, no?" approach to asking.

When I was first hired, my company was employing around three hundred people. Not big, but not small. Within the first year, I met regularly with the Director of Research and Development (R&D), the Chief Technology Officer (CTO), and the CEO. How was I able to secure time from everyone in my chain of command? I just asked. That's right, all I did was ask if I could meet with them. This same approach will work for you, too. Never talk yourself out of a great mentor simply because you *think* they'll say no. Some will, but some won't. If they say no, it's typically not because anything is wrong with you personally. Most likely, it's because of schedule conflicts or other time constraints. It costs nothing to ask, and the potential payoff is *huge*.

Reading is valuable, but no interactive conversations take place while reading. Asking questions of someone face-to-face allows you to zero in on specific topics and keep hammering away at them until you feel like you have the answer you're looking for, or you at least have more direction. After a mentor gets to know you better, they can steer you based on previous conversations you've had. There is no substitute for mentoring when it comes to the specificity of the guidance you can receive.

If you have someone specific in mind to be your mentor, ask. If you don't have someone specific in mind, ask your manager for suggestions. Many companies *require* their people managers to help in this regard. You're doing them a favor by proactively giving them specifics on *how* they can help you.

Remember the Opportunity Tree from an earlier chapter? Mentorship allows you to quickly add more vetted branches to your tree and learn valuable personal and career shortcuts in the process. I can't tell you how many helpful insights I've gained through meeting with people who have experienced more success in certain areas of life than I have. Just the book references alone have been worth the effort. You never know what future opportunities will come from your connections to others, so do your best to build out the biggest, fullest tree you can by finding a quality mentor.

IF YOU'VE EVER CONSIDERED BEING A MENTOR, DO IT

Maturing is a process, part of which *should* be getting to a place where you put an emphasis on giving back to those who don't know or have as much as you do. When personal success begins to feel hollow, activities like mentoring can reinvigorate you.

Many parts of life need balance. If you put too much emphasis on one thing, including yourself, it can throw other areas out of whack. Sadly, some people are so self-focused their entire lives that they miss out on one of the key ways to positively impact others, and in the end, their own happiness. Helping others adds balance to your life.

If you've reached a point where you think mentoring might be an interesting endeavor, you should seriously consider pursuing it. The only requirement is that you have a legitimate desire to want to help. You don't need to know what you are doing when you start, either—you'll pick up many of the details as you go. You also may think you won't know what to talk about or that you're not great with people, but don't talk yourself out of a great opportunity before even trying.

Any time you do something new, it's a little scary. You're not alone.

Pain often accompanies growth because it means you're engaging in activities you haven't already mastered. Don't let fear keep you from doing what might be one of the most fruitful endeavors you've pursued in years. The more you mentor people, the easier it becomes.

There's a common thread to the backstory of nearly every great teacher or public speaker I admire: They were all *terrible* in the beginning. Almost without exception, nearly every single one of them says they were awful teachers and speakers when they started, but they didn't let that stop them. How fortunate for us that they didn't! If someone like John C. Maxwell, a leadership author and teacher, gave up because of poor initial performance, millions of people would have been robbed of his teaching gifts.

One author and teacher I listen to regularly says he was so introverted when he first started, he couldn't even look someone in the face and talk. This is coming from a person who has literally changed my life. Seeing how far he has come gives me hope that I, too, can become significantly better at teaching, speaking, and mentoring.

From a selfish standpoint, mentoring others is an excellent way to stand out from your peers. Write this down on a sticky note and put it on your computer monitor: People who stop making everything about themselves shine like a lightsaber in a dark room. The world is teeming with people only interested in their own personal happiness and gain. To make a name for yourself in a group of people who operate a routine way, act differently. People with resources actively look for others with whom to entrust their resources. Selflessness is a key character trait that qualifies us for further advancement. If you are already a gifted engineer, investing in other people lifts you even higher above your peers.

You've probably heard it said that if you want to see if you truly know something, teach it. Teaching causes you to question ideas and concepts you thought you were settled on a long time ago. As a result, you may learn far more about yourself and your profession by explaining the material to someone else. Mentoring can aid in your own personal growth because you approach topics from another person's perspective and explain ideas and concepts in a way that's engaging to your listeners.

Parents know how children can ask simple questions that can be very hard to answer. Questions about how birds fly can be remarkably difficult to answer if you've never done a thorough investigation into it yourself. As an adult, you may have stopped being impressed by the world you live in. Kids, on the other hand, are discovering things for the first time and haven't lost that zeal to figure out how things work. Mentoring opens new avenues of discovery and reignites your passion for learning and sharing as you help others through the learning process.

Depending on the size of the place you work, you may already have a formal mentorship program. Throw your hat in the ring and volunteer to help. If there is not an existing mentorship program, start one. It's no more difficult than telling your manager you think your co-workers could benefit significantly from having a mentorship program, and you'd like to help make that happen. Because of your desire, you might get the opportunity to work with the Human Resources Department to craft an official program. If not, maybe you can create an informal program at a team level to prove that it will work. The point is that you see the importance of mentorship, and you're willing to put your time and energy behind your conviction.

TIPS FOR BEING A GREAT MENTOR

The single most important tip for current or future mentors is this: Take time to establish a rapport with the person you're mentoring. Get to know them with the intent of gaining their trust. What is their real passion in life? What do they see themselves doing in five years? What do they like to do in their spare time? Doing this expands your pool of allowable future topics using questions most anyone would consider normal. You aren't trying to pry into their personal lives, just getting to know them better so you can create a safe environment in which to help more effectively.

Let your mentee know that you volunteered for the role. No one threatened or cajoled you into being a mentor, and as such, you *want* to help. This communicates to the individual that they aren't an afterthought—you're expecting to spend time with them answering questions and sharing information you learned over the course of your career. They don't have to worry about being a nuisance, you've already told them it's OK to periodically interrupt you.

When you first meet with your mentee, establish basic objectives and guidelines. For instance, how often should you meet? Weekly? Monthly? What about times outside of the formal scheduled mentorship meetings? Are you available any time, or would you like to set up specific mentoring hours like office hours for college professors? Doing this alleviates anxiety on the part of the mentee because they can then depend on those times to safely engage with you without feeling like they are interrupting your work.

When setting up mentoring sessions, do your best to create a safe environment. For example, schedule a location that's quiet and safe from eavesdropping. If necessary, move the session off-site and hold it at a quiet coffee shop or restaurant. You aren't *trying* to have a deep discussion, but you want an environment that will support one if that's the direction a mentoring session takes.

As a mentor, you may be asked questions that people don't feel comfortable asking anyone else. For example, you may get a question like, "I don't understand why my manager is acting this way, did I do something wrong?" Make it as easy as possible to ask and answer those questions. If a sensitive topic comes up, like friction with a co-worker or manager, the discussion *must* stay between the two of you. Promote this free flow of information by creating a safe environment.

It is also important to let your new mentee know what topics are open for discussion. Do you want to keep the sessions focused solely on technical material related to their job? Are you comfortable fielding questions in other areas like finance, leadership, or interpersonal communication? You have to decide what areas you feel comfortable with when mentoring. This is your time to help, and if you think you have more to offer than just engineering wisdom, why not open the conversations a little more?

Many problems at work are symptoms of problems in other areas of a person's life. You're probably not a clinical psychologist and aren't qualified to address significant problems such as drug abuse and depression, but you *can* speak to many common issues engineers face with authority, such as the importance of good character, time management, and proper work-life balance. These aren't directly tied to technical work but are very important to the overall happiness and productivity of an engineer. Connecting with someone in a more significant way gives you the right to speak to these other areas which may positively impact their professional performance and overall quality of life. The work-life balance strategies that have worked for you may work for the individual you're mentoring as well.

If I could travel back in time and talk to my 22-year-old self, most of my advice would have nothing to do with engineering. I'd tell myself how to be a better friend and husband, how to better deal with family problems, and the importance of getting involved in organizations that focus on helping others. You can share this same advice *right now* with the people you are mentoring. You can figuratively travel back in time for them. Share with them what *you* wish you would have known ten, twenty, or thirty years ago. Odds are, they'd like to know, too.

To get the most out of the mentoring sessions, prepare the material you want to cover ahead of time. Rather than winging it, your sessions should be focused and structured to get the most out of your time together. If you plan on covering the dynamics between technical workers and management, come with material ahead of time that you've put some thought into. You want to avoid showing up and staring at each other for an hour. The last thing you want is for either party to dread mentoring sessions. If that's happening repeatedly, you may as well cancel the whole thing and do something more productive.

SUMMARY

- Your influence is the only thing that outlives you.

- Engineers leave companies because they are unable to connect with others. Mentorship is an easy way to create camaraderie between people.

- Everyone can learn from someone more successful than themselves. If you don't have a mentor, get one.

- Helping someone else is a surefire way to grow yourself. If you've ever considered being a mentor, do it.

- Make it your first priority to build a rapport with the engineer you're mentoring. Trust is foundational to being able to influence another person.

- Treat your mentoring sessions like they are important because they are. Come prepared.

Conclusion

You did it! You made it all the way to the back of the book. As an author, I never take that for granted, given how many other voices are vying for your attention throughout your busy day. I'm honored and humbled that you would spend some of your time with me to grow and stretch yourself in the area of people skills.

As engineers, it's easy to undervalue human dynamics, thinking people skills would be nice to learn when time allows or after we're doing everything else correctly. This thinking is backward. A healthy people environment is the foundation of any endeavor our teams will ever undertake. While we may experience a certain amount of success through raw technical horsepower, how many unnecessary relational problems will we cause in the process?

From an engineering standpoint, people skills have been drastically downplayed, probably due to a combination of the personalities that typically choose engineering professions and the lack of information in this area that specifically targets engineers. Because of this, engineers gravitate toward what everyone else seems to value, usually their technical ability, and that throws them out of balance. They miss countless opportunities *every day* to impact the effectiveness of their teams from a relational perspective.

Mark my words: *Failings with people can be the undoing of even the most talented technical team.* We need to change our mindset when it comes to people skills. Instead of viewing ourselves as strictly solid technical resources, we can begin viewing what we do as a dual profession with a focus on both team building *and* engineering. We don't have to pick one; we can do both.

Look for ways to apply the material in this book. Learn the names of your co-workers. Assess your interpersonal bank accounts with those around you. Do your best to create the most productive and effective psychologically safe team in your company. Don't dismiss the idea because it's not technical in nature. The results are undeniable.

You are responsible for the culture of your team. If you work in an adversarial environment where bad blood between individuals is the norm, it's because individuals are not owning up to their responsibilities as team members. You can be the first person to put a stake in the ground and decide you're going to operate on a higher level than those around you. Use your influence to show people a better way.

As a teacher of this material, I have the benefit of always having the concepts in this book on my mind, which makes it easier for me to put them into practice. You may not be so lucky, and you may be tempted to immediately revert back to your old ways of interacting with people as soon as you put the book down. Don't do it! Pick an idea or concept that resonated with you the most and start doing it until you begin seeing the fruits of your change. Don't get discouraged along the way. This is a life change, and there will be setbacks.

Look around you. For better or for worse, this is your life. Are you making the impact you want? If not, it's time for a change. While very exciting for a short period of time, personal success may leave you unsatisfied and wanting more, like a drug or alcohol addiction. The only thing that provides long-term satisfaction is helping other people. You have opportunities every day to have a real, tangible effect on the quality of life of those around you. You can help people, and in turn, help yourself lead a life of more significance and satisfaction.

Afterword

I'd love to hear from you. If you liked the book, have any suggestions for how to make the material better, or would like to contact me about my availability as a speaker or instructor, you can reach me at:

Website: www.peopleskillsforengineers.com
Email: peopleskillsforengineers@gmail.com

If you found this book valuable, I encourage you to share it with someone else. You can help get this information out to as many engineers as possible and start changing the culture at your workplace from the inside out. Additionally, please consider submitting an online review to compel others to read it as well.

Bibliography

Bettger, Frank. *How I Raised Myself from Failure to Success in Selling.* New York: Touchstone, Imprint of Simon & Schuster, 1947.

Bolton, Robert. *People Skills: How to Assert Yourself, Listen to Others, and Resolve Conflicts.* New York: Simon & Schuster, 1986.

Branagan, Alison. *Making Sense of Business: A No-Nonsense Guide to Business Skills.* New York: Korgan Page, Publisher, 2009. p. 136. J. Paul Getty cited.

Carnegie, Dale. *How to Win Friends and Influence People.* Simon & Schuster hard cover ed. New York: Simon & Schuster, 2009.

Collins, Jim. *Good to Great: Why Some Companies Make the Leap and Others Don't.* New York: HarperCollins, 2001.

Covey, Stephen R. *The 7 Habits of Highly Effective People: Powerful Lessons in Personal Change.* Free Press trade paperback ed. New York: Simon & Schuster, 2004.

Eastman, Blake. "How Much of Communication Is Really Nonverbal?" The Nonverbal Group. Article published August 2011. http://www.nonverbalgroup.com/2011/08/how-much-of-communication-is-really-nonverbal.

Giblin, Les. *How to Have Confidence and Power in Dealing with People.* New York: Prentice Hall Press, 1956.

Giblin, Les. *Skill with People.* Rev. ed. 2010.

Goleman, Daniel. *Emotional Intelligence.* Bantam trade paperback ed. 1997. New York: Bantam Books, 1997.

Goleman, Daniel. "Help Young Talent Develop a Professional Mindset." Article published September 13, 2015. www.danielgoleman.info/daniel-goleman-help-young-talent-develop-a-professional-mindset/.

"Graduate's Social and Emotional Skills in the Workplace." Accessed July 11, 2018. www.haygroup.com/en/our-library/infographics/graduates-social-and-emotional-skills-in-the-workplace/.

Hendricksen, Dave. *12 Essential Skills for Software Architects.* Upper Saddle River, NJ: Addison-Wesley, 2011.

Hill, Napoleon. *Think and Grow Rich.* Meriden, CT: Ralston Society, 1937.

"How Stress Affects Your Body and Behavior." Mayo Clinic, Mayo Foundation for Medical Education and Research. Article published April 28, 2016. www.mayoclinic.org/healthy-lifestyle/stress-management/in-depth/stress-symptoms/art-20050987.

"J. Paul Getty." Peanuts—Wikiquote. Accessed July 11, 2018. en.wikiquote.org/wiki/J._Paul_Getty/.

Jeffress, Robert. *When Forgiveness Doesn't Make Sense.* Colorado Springs, CO: WaterBrook Press, 2000.

Kogon, Kory, Suzette Blakemore, and James Wood. *Project Management for the Unofficial Project Manager.* Dallas, TX: BenBella Books, 2015.

Lebowitz, Shana. "Google Considers This to Be the Most Critical Trait of Successful Teams." Business Insider. Article published November 20, 2015. www.businessinsider.com/amy-edmondson-on-psychological-safety-2015-11.

Maxwell, John C. *The 5 Levels of Leadership.* New York: Center Street, Hachette Book Group, 2013.

Maxwell, John C. *The 21 Irrefutable Laws of Leadership.* Nashville, TN: Thomas Nelson, 2007.

Navarro, Joe, and Marvin Karlins. *What Every BODY Is Saying: An Ex-FBI Agent's Guide to Speed-Reading People.* New York: HarperCollins Publishers, 2008.

Patterson, K., J. Grenny, R. McMillen, and A. Switzler. *Crucial Conversations: Tools for Talking When Stakes Are High.* McGraw-Hill, 2012.

"Re:Work—Guide: Understand Team Effectiveness." Google. Accessed July 11, 2018. rework.withgoogle.com/guides/understanding-team-effectiveness/steps/introduction.

Schwartz, David J. *The Magic of Thinking Big.* Prentice-Hall, Inc., 1959.

Sinek, S. *Start with Why: How Great Leaders Inspire Everyone to Take Action.* New York. Penguin Group, 2011.

"The Effects of Stress on Your Body." Healthline Media. Accessed July 11, 2018. www.healthline.com/health/stress/effects-on-body/.

"The Effects of Stress on Your Body." WebMD. Accessed July 11, 2018. www.